Ulsterbus & Citybus 1988–2003
The Hesketh Years
BUSES IN ULSTER VOLUME 6

G Irvine Millar
with foreword by Ted Hesketh

Ted Hesketh, CBE

Born in Larne, Ted attended the local grammar school before going to Queen's University where he took a science degree.

After a period with Shorts, the aircraft and missile manufacturer, Ted joined Ulsterbus in 1971 and was encouraged to study for his qualification in accountancy. Initially following a financial career with Ulsterbus, he later broadened into general management, becoming Managing Director of Citybus and Ulsterbus in 1988. In 1995 he was also appointed Managing Director of Northern Ireland Railways and led the integration with the bus companies to form Translink. He was made a Commander of the Order of the British Empire (CBE) in the 2002 Queen's Birthday Honours List, for services to public transport. He retired from the bus and railway companies in 2003.

Ted was the first person from Northern Ireland to be elected National President of the Confederation of Passenger Transport (UK), and went on to become Vice President of UITP, the international public transport body.

He is married with one son and lives in Co Antrim.

Ted Hesketh wearing the Presidential chain of the Confederation of Passenger Transport (UK)

All rights reserved. No part of this publication may be reproduced, stored in a retrieval system or transmitted in any form or by any means, electronic, mechanical, photocopying, scanning, recording or otherwise, without the prior written permission of the copyright owners and publisher of this book.

6 5 4 3 2 1

© G Irvine Millar and Colourpoint Books 2006

Designed by Colourpoint Books, Newtownards
Printed by W&G Baird Ltd

ISBN 10: 1 904242 28 6
ISBN 13: 978 1 904242 28 4

Colourpoint Books are grateful for the generous support given by Translink in the production of this book.

Colourpoint Books
Colourpoint House,
Jubilee Business Park
21 Jubilee Road
NEWTOWNARDS
Northern Ireland
BT23 4YH
Tel: 028 9182 0505
Fax: 028 9182 1900
E-mail: info@colourpoint.co.uk
Web-site: www.colourpoint.co.uk

Irvine Millar, a native of Edinburgh, has a wealth of experience in public transport and buses, both from a professional and 'enthusiast' perspective. Moving from London Transport, in 1967 he joined Ulsterbus, with whom he was to be employed until his retirement in 2001, serving successively as PA to the Managing Director, Projects Manager and Inspector General. Irvine's work, however, has also been his hobby, and to his credit can be listed numerous articles for *Buses Illustrated*, *Bus & Coach* and *Buses*, as well as the commemorative publication *50 Years of Public Transport*. He was also the author of Volume 4 in this series, *Ulsterbus 1967–1988, The Heubeck Years*. Irvine also co-compiles the Fleet News Ireland column for *Buses* magazine. He is married, with two grown-up children, and lives in Belfast.

Front cover: Downpatrick-allocated Mk IV Goldliner No 1629 heads south from Belfast on the Ormeau Road en route to its home base in June 2000. This Plaxton Premier-bodied Volvo B10M was new in 1996. Coincidentally, the previous No 1629, a Bristol LH6L bus, now in preservation with the Irish Transport Trust, had also been allocated to the Co Down town.   *Raymond Bell*

Back cover
Top: In 2000, four Mercedes O405GN articulated buses were delivered for use on the *City Express* services to Newtownabbey via the M2/M5 motorways. No 3102 was caught by the photographer in Royal Avenue in August that year. The livery applied to these vehicles was quite restrained when compared with previous deliveries for *City Express* work.
Norman Johnston

Bottom: No 890 is one of the third batch of Wrights TS-bodied Mercedes 709D midibuses purchased by Ulsterbus. Delivered in 1993, it was photographed the following year at the 'Super Shelter' provided by Ulsterbus at the then-new Antrim Area Hospital.   *Author*

CONTENTS

Foreword......................................4
Preface and acknowledgements 5
Ulsterbus and Citybus Operations 1988–1995.......6
The Spectre of Privatisation 12
Translink Operations 1996–2003 13
The March of Technology 14
Bus Priority..................................14
Business Review.............................20
The Fleets 21
The Search for New Identities 30
Special Events...............................33

Photo sections
    The Fleet in 1988......................34
    New vehicles 1989–2003 52
    Pre-owned vehicles acquired 1989–2003 ...89
    Touring Coaches 115
    Goldline.............................122
    Belfast–Dublin Express.................131
    Airbus 135
    Service Vehicles......................138
    Premises............................143
    Demonstrators 155
    Company people 165

Ulsterbus and Citybus Managers 1988–2003......167
Fleet list....................................169

Foreword

by Ted Hesketh, CBE
Former Managing Director, Translink

This is the sixth book in the 'Buses in Ulster' series published by Colourpoint Books. They are to be congratulated for bringing the story of Ulsterbus and Citybus to a wider audience, and putting it on record for future generations.

During the first two decades of the 'Troubles', the men and women of Ulsterbus and Citybus had to cope with unprecedented difficulties. My predecessor, Werner Heubeck, gave outstanding leadership when it would have been so easy to throw in the towel. To keep buses running normally was the top priority and everything else was secondary.

My early days with Ulsterbus were focussed on keeping the finances in good order when buses were being destroyed in quantity; compensation was a thorny issue, and revenues were subject to frequent disruption. Gradually, as Mr Heubeck's deputy, I took on additional responsibilities such as industrial tribunals, property development, etc; Mr Heubeck gave me a lot of scope in the day to day running of the business so the transition to Managing Director was relatively smooth.

The worst of the 'Troubles' had passed when I became MD in 1988. Even so, this volume records nearly 250 buses totally destroyed by terrorism during my time as MD. Thankfully no staff were killed. In 1996, we erected a ceramic wall panel in Laganside Buscentre to commemorate the twelve busmen killed earlier in the 'Troubles'. With the passage of time it is very pleasing that the heroism of our bus drivers, and all the staff who supported them during the 'Troubles', is increasingly recognised. I hope that in time there will be a more substantial memorial for those killed and injured, which will also record the bravery of the very many who, on a daily basis, displayed great courage to maintain services throughout the 'Troubles'.

Like most bus companies, Ulsterbus faced declining passenger numbers due to the growth in private car usage. Introduction of a market led approach saw the development of many new services, real improvements to the quality of all services and much better public information.

Strenuous efforts went into creating a new climate of industrial relations, and this helped avoid unnecessary service disruptions. There was increasing recognition that many of our staff work unsocial hours which can impact on family life. By way of "thank you" we ran a series of Family Fun Days for partners and children – hugely enjoyed by all !

A previously untold success story was the effective blocking of proposals to privatise and deregulate bus services in the Province. These proposals were wholly unsuited to Northern Ireland and had they succeeded there is little doubt that Ulsterbus, as we know it, would no longer exist.

As always there is unfinished business. The E-way and Super-route busway schemes are long term projects conceived during the period covered by this book. Less well known are similar schemes going into north and west Belfast. Some of the land currently blighted by the peace line offers a unique opportunity to develop a new busway to benefit the entire community. I hope that future volumes of 'Buses in Ulster' will be able to carry reports of substantial progress on these schemes.

I am proud to have played a part in the history of these two great companies. From retirement, I look back with fondness to a most enjoyable time working in both Ulsterbus and Citybus with some of the best professionals in the business. Despite all the problems and the long hours we still managed to have some fun!

From the start of Ulsterbus in 1967 until he retired in 2001, Irvine Millar was a valued member of the senior management. During the period of this volume he developed his initial role as management auditor, to create a specialism embracing the whole area of bus priority measures. He even managed to convince some of our colleagues in Road Service that building more roads is not necessarily the best answer to every traffic problem, and that sometimes public transport has a role to play! Irvine's extensive knowledge of buses has been put to good use in this book. He goes beyond the detailed recording of fleet changes to trace the history of service development and touches on many other aspects of Ulsterbus and Citybus to the reader's benefit and it is with great pleasure that I commend it to you.

Ted Hesketh
Antrim
November 2006

Preface and acknowledgements

In the preface to my previous book (Buses in Ulster Vol 4 – *The Heubeck Years*), I gave a brief summary of my career and responsibilities within the company. When Ted Hesketh took over from Werner Heubeck at the end of 1988 he implemented some reorganisation of responsibilities for senior managers. I was given the new title of Inspector General, and although retaining responsibility for the fleet, my new duties concentrated upon a progressive Management Audit of the District units, scrutinising both their efficiency and the quality of their operations. Responsiveness to local market needs became a focus of the new regime, so I was able to make constructive recommendations relating to routes, frequencies and timetables, many of which were adopted, as well as criticisms, if they were needed, on the cleanliness and maintenance of the fleet and premises. I also became very involved in the relatively new aspect of traffic engineering known as 'bus priority', which required extensive liaison with the staff of the Roads Service of the Department of the Environment (later Department for Regional Development). While these topics may be somewhat esoteric to readers with a more focussed interest in buses, I hope that some flavour of the progress which was made over these important and formative years for public transport in Northern Ireland will come across in this volume.

This volume differs from earlier volumes in the series in combining the presentation of Ulsterbus and Citybus developments over the period. Although the common management of the fleets started back in 1973, the two systems continued to grow together until the visible standardisation and interchangeability achieved during the 1990s which justifies the position presented in this volume. I hope that I have achieved a fair balance of emphasis for each of the operations.

The volume also covers two quite distinct phases of corporate organisation, before and after the reorganisation of public transport 'delivery' in 1995/6, which was imposed upon the companies involved by the government departments. As far as possible I have tried to present a background explanation of these changes as well as comment upon the consequences, not least to fleet renewal. As these developments are still very recent and personal, it is difficult to take the broad and dispassionate view which one should take in describing history. Perhaps by the time another volume in the history of Ulster's principal bus companies is due to be written, the success, or otherwise, of the Translink 'integration' saga will have become clearer.

I would like to express my sincere thanks to the many friends and colleagues who have contributed material, or assistance, for this volume. Ted Hesketh has contributed an excellent Foreword, and has also contributed suggestions on some of the most important developments from his inside knowledge of the highest management echelons. Once again I thank John Montgomery for allowing access to official fleet records, and other colleagues for whom my voice from retirement must have seemed like that of a ghost from days of yore.

I thank the Irish Transport Trust, especially its Hon Chairman, Will Hughes, for his compilation of the fleet records, and the photographers who have willingly loaned a huge range of photographs from which I have made the selection which appears in this volume, all of which hopefully have been individually and correctly credited.

I would also thank Keith Moffatt, who has succeeded Ted Hesketh in the top seat of the Translink management structure, for his generous support to enable this book to be produced in full colour, worthy of the high standards attained by our bus operations throughout the Hesketh era, and to wish Translink, and their new creation, Metro, which has supplanted Citybus in the public perception, every success in developing and expanding patronage of our public bus services.

Once again, I acknowledge the forbearance of my wife Irene, whose eager anticipation of the completion of this volume, has been no less, though for different reasons, than our loyal readership.

G Irvine Millar
Belfast
November 2006

Ulsterbus and Citybus Operations 1988–1995

When Ted Hesketh took over from Werner Heubeck as Managing Director of Ulsterbus and Citybus at the end of 1988, it was clear that the companies needed a change of direction. For over twenty-one years in Ulsterbus (fifteen years in Citybus) the companies had battled successfully against quite exceptional adversities to maintain their established network of public services to be available for the public to use. In his first address to the companies' management team, Mr Hesketh questioned whether that network was, in fact, what the public still wanted to be able to use. The theme was to let the market lead our operations, rather than vice-versa. Market research and positive marketing were to be used much more extensively than before to re-launch the image of the companies and their products before the public.

A year earlier, the Government minister Richard Needham had instructed the Board of Ulsterbus that they should be competing vigorously with the railway. Although common management of buses and trains had ended with dismantling of the Ulster Transport Authority in 1966/7, both systems remained under the common ownership of the Northern Ireland Transport Holding Company. Although free to develop its bus operations independently of railway control, the Ulsterbus policy after 1967 had not included 'head on' competition with trains.

Nevertheless, the thinking behind the letter did influence company and departmental policy during the next few years, leading in particular to development of the Belfast–Dublin service and introduction of the Goldline Express concept, including the Belfast–Londonderry *Maiden City Flyer*. It was nearly a decade before the move toward 'integration' of bus and train services emerged.

CITYBUS

It was recognised that Citybus operations needed the most urgent attention. Although the heavy losses sustained by Belfast Corporation had been largely turned around, the company returns were still not fully satisfactory. Citybus was the only major bus undertaking in the UK operating the continental flat fare system, introduced in April 1978. Pre-purchased multi-journey tickets were cancelled by passengers on boarding. Features of the system laid it open to passenger fraud, which surveys indicated might be costing around 14% of revenue. This nettle was grasped at once, with the responsibility for checking and cancelling tickets reverting to the drivers in November 1988. Within weeks, revenue had increased, not by 14% but by 25%!

Vandalism and smoking were also successfully tackled. In compensation to the passenger, an immediate start was made in improving passenger facilities on the buses. The standard 32 seat plus 47 standing layout of the Bristol RELLs was improved to 43 seats with 34 standing. Furthermore, more than 50% of the seating capacity of the Bristols was changed from utilitarian, solid fibreglass to fully upholstered seating, trimmed in moquette. The first new buses, Leyland Tigers with Alexander 'Q' bodies, were 'fully seated' 51-seaters with 22 standing, while a later batch even had the more comfortable 'semi-luxury' seating specified for Ulsterbus.

BUS STOPS

One of the first campaigns throughout the Province was a major purge on the condition of bus stop signs. The value of this was widely questioned, but as fixed stops are the visible evidence of the existence of a transport service, even when there is no bus in sight, it is hardly surprising that a damaged or shabby stop sign reflects badly on the operator responsible. A related area of improvement was in the display of service information at bus stops. Ulsterbus had not previously deemed this cost effective, but in the new regime it became an important measure in promoting services to the potential customers.

CORPORATE IMAGE

Steps were also taken to upgrade the corporate image presentations, in fleet livery, lettering, logo style, and special product branding. These measures are described more fully on page 30.

MINIBUS SERVICES

The introduction of higher frequencies, using small minibuses, had become a very widespread feature of public transport in Great Britain during the 1980s, largely as a response to the threats or opportunities of deregulation, introduced in 1986. As Northern Ireland did not have that legislative change, Ulsterbus had been less active in adopting that type of operation. However the value of that type of vehicle for developing new services in urban and suburban areas was recognised, especially in residential areas where full-size buses might not be workable, or socially acceptable. Thus, minibus town services had been started in Bangor

In 1990 a minibus service was introduced in parts of North and West Belfast using Mercedes No 807, painted in this very simple red Citybus scheme. Two circular routes, numbered 74A and 74B, were operated between Highfield Estate and Stewarts supermarket on the Ballygomartin Road and from Stewarts to Crimea Street on the Shankill Road. The operation wasn't a success and was withdrawn after several months.

Paul Savage

Mercedes 709D/Wrights TS No 825 is shown in *Busybus* livery but lettered for the *University Link* service between the Queen's area and Jordanstown. Demand for the service rapidly outgrew the small buses and, in 2006, it is operated mainly with double-deckers.

Richard Whitford

in autumn 1987 and in several other towns during 1988, and small buses took over the *Airbus* service in the same year. With the adoption of the *Busybus* brand name and a brighter livery, together with superior vehicles, with 25 seats in coachbuilt bodies, this type of service spread rapidly throughout the Province. By 1993 *Busybus* services had started in Bangor, Newtownards, Donaghadee, Comber, Downpatrick, Newcastle, Ballynahinch, Dundonald, Holywood, Dunmurry, Ballymena, Lisburn, Newry, Banbridge, Antrim, Ballyclare, Larne, Whitehead, Coleraine, Portrush, Ballycastle, Omagh, Londonderry, Dungannon, and Enniskillen. Independent operators had secured licences in 1989 to operate similar town services in Ballymoney and Strabane, although the latter was absorbed by Ulsterbus in 1990.

Moreover, small buses had launched *University Link* services between the Queen's area of Belfast and Jordanstown NUU campus, and between Coleraine NUU campus and Portstewart and Portrush. These *Unilink* services were long overdue responses to known passenger needs. In both cases, demand rapidly outgrew the capacity of the small buses, which were soon replaced by full-size single-deckers, and ultimately by double-deckers.

GOLDLINE

The widespread network of limited stop services which Ulsterbus had established across the Province, had been marketed under the brand 'Ulsterbus Express' introduced in 1978, but so many vehicles carried this fleet name and were used on ordinary services that the brand image had lost its significance. Accordingly steps were taken to re-launch the network with a new 'Goldline' brand image, new 'Goldliner' coaches offering new standards of comfort, and some new services and improved frequencies. The 'Goldline' name had been the proposal of the late Sam Dowling, Northern Area Manager.

The flagship route, christened the *Maiden City Flyer*, was an entirely new service between the Province's two largest cities, Londonderry and Belfast over the direct Glenshane road, which had been extensively improved over the previous decade, but whose potential as a route had not been grasped by Ulsterbus management. Introduction of this route under the new regime was to prove the most remarkable success story of the period under review, though by no means the only one. The initial timetable in April 1990 had two round trips a day, which allowed for people to spend a working day in Belfast. A third round trip was added quickly, followed by two more to give a two hourly frequency, in 1991. Such was the public response to this service that frequency soon became hourly,

Three of the Alexander 'TE'-bodied Leyland Tigers are seen in Londonderry at the Goldline relaunch. Area Manager Andy Watt and Depot Manager David Leathem pose with Tigers Nos 522–4.
Ulsterbus

and more recently generally half hourly but with a departure every fifteen minutes in peak periods.

The outstanding success of the Goldline re-launch, and of the 'Flyer' did much to convince management to explore other opportunities for development and improvement of services whose pattern and public popularity had been dormant for several years. Other Goldline routes to be individually branded included *Orchard Express* to Armagh, *Lakeland Express* to Enniskillen, *Atlantic Coast Express* to Coleraine and Portrush and the *Antrim Coaster*.

BELFAST – DUBLIN

Although the HMS Catherwood company had introduced a through Belfast–Dublin express coach service in 1927, this ceased in 1933 with state ownership, which was unashamedly designed to support the railways and suppress competition. Ulsterbus had tried on several occasions since 1967 to secure an operating licence for this route, but even the introduction of EEC cross-border licensing procedures in 1973 failed to release the railways' stranglehold. However a licence was at last awarded in 1989 and a joint service with Bus Éireann was successfully introduced. The original timetable of three journeys a day has been expanded, although growth was slower than on the 'Flyer'. It proved impossible to devise a politically non-controversial branding for this route, but the success of the Goldline brand soon spread to cross-border as well as internal routes, corresponding to Bus Éireann's *Expressway* image.

ANTRIM COASTER

Another service which was to receive special marketing effort was the *Antrim Coaster*, the once daily summer service round the world famous Antrim Coast Road from Belfast via Carrickfergus, Larne and Carnlough to Cushendall, Cushendun, Ballycastle and the Causeway Coast resorts. By doubling frequency to two daily and promoting the route as one of the classic coach journeys of the world, patronage was increased by 47% in a single season.

CITY EXPRESS

This was an exciting new concept, basically an express service connecting the outer suburbs of Newtownabbey (built as city overspill) with the city centre, using an existing motorway whose potential for relatively local commuter use had been all but ignored by previous management. The route was facilitated with some modest bus priority measures to bypass the daily congestion at the city end of the motorway. Above all the service was designed as a demonstration of the quality of public transport which could be achieved with congestion free exclusive busway infrastructure in the future. It was sufficiently successful after its first year to warrant investment in a new fleet of coaches and a new brand image.

FARE DEAL

A second major revision of the fares structure and ticketing system in Belfast came in 1991, with the launch of the 'Fare Deal' for Belfast and Newtownabbey. Within Belfast, a new Inner Zone was created, with a lower flat fare for journeys wholly within the zone or as an add-on to City Zone journeys. This was beneficial to passengers making journeys across the city centre to reach destinations such as the three major hospitals, Queens University and the two railway stations, which were included in the 'Inner Zone'. At the same time the facility of free transfer in the City Centre to complete such journeys, which had been widely abused, was withdrawn, but passengers could now pay their cross town fares on boarding their first bus.

A range of office issue Travel Cards offering unlimited travel within the City Zone (Gold Card) within one of three sectors (Silver Cards) was also introduced, as was a driver-issued Day Ticket allowing unlimited travel within the City Zone after 09.30 (all day on Saturday and Sunday).

For many years there had been a serious anomaly for passengers travelling between Newtownabbey and Belfast. Those who could use Citybus routes via Glengormley had had the benefit of the Belfast flat fare, for journeys markedly longer than to other Citybus termini, while those who used the Ulsterbus routes via Merville had to pay the mileage related fare. This was resolved by introducing a 'Newtownabbey Zone' with a uniform flat fare between all Newtownabbey stages and the Belfast City Zone. The zone boundary was fixed at Bellevue on the Antrim Road and at Abbey Centre on the Shore Road. Whilst the fare across this boundary was higher than the former Citybus flat fare, it was cheaper than the mileage related fare payable on Ulsterbus routes.

Short distance fares were retained within the Newtownabbey Zone, which was beneficial to passengers using Citybus routes who had previously had to pay the Belfast flat fare for short journeys such as between Carnmoney and Glengormley.

TICKET SYSTEMS

The installation of Wayfarer electronic ticket registers at four Ulsterbus depots in 1989/90 and in Citybus in 1991 completed the conversion of the entire Ulsterbus and Citybus fleet.

STAGE SERVICES

Local bus services around the Province were still being maintained on a reliable basis, without the crises in, for example, rural services which characterised the bus industry in Great Britain. Transport of school pupils continued to be of vital importance in determining the peak commitments of staff and vehicles in Ulsterbus. However 'other revenue' reflected the national decline of 2–3% per annum. The companies therefore explored every opportunity, even in rural areas, to entice passengers back to buses. Experiments with new routes and timings were characteristic. Some were short-lived, such as Markethill–Richhill; others survived, such as Cushendall–Ballycastle and Lisburn–Drumbo.

SUPPORT FOR PUBLIC TRANSPORT

During this period there was very little support given by Government to public transport in Northern Ireland. In a comparison with Great Britain in 1989/90, it was revealed that support per head of population was only 25% of the GB level; support per mile was only 29%. The effect was that Northern Ireland passenger fares had to cover 96% of total costs, while in Great Britain the figure was only 76%. Nevertheless the level of fares was comparable and the level of service available, allowing for lower population density and other factors was only slightly below GB standards.

GOLDLINE REVIEW

A major review of progress on the development of Goldline Express services was undertaken in 1994/5. Most of the timetable improvements envisaged by this review were implemented during the following months. Other measures proposed included the concentration of all Goldline services into Europa Buscentre in Belfast, to facilitate interchange for passengers making cross-Province journeys. Ten years were to pass before this was implemented by a very different management team! Other ideas examined which have not materialised were a 'hub' interchange system at Dungannon with east–west services making two hourly connections with new services to the north and south of the Province; and appointment of a 'brand manager' to monitor the quality standards associated with the network and to organise various 'added value' schemes. The review also identified towns and potential routes around the Province which were not served by the Goldline network and examined how these might be added to the network.

The Spectre of Privatisation

In the late 1980s it was government policy, driven by the Treasury in London, that the companies should be privatised. A plan was developed by Chairman Bill Bradshaw and Ted Hesketh to put forward an employee buy-out led by the existing management. However, because of the security situation, the idea of privatisation did not then proceed. The Treasury persisted however, ensuring that several expensive consultants were employed to review the pattern of ownership and regulation. Although the Board of Directors were neutral to the principle of privatisation, they did have a professional responsibility to appraise the politicians and civil servants of the likely outcomes of the methodologies they were considering.

By then the weaknesses of the schemes implemented in Great Britain were very apparent. In particular there was criticism of the ease by which managers who had bought out their companies could sell out to the emerging large groups, making millionaires on a regular basis. Some of the groups were noted for the extent of their asset stripping. All three of the largest groups had made approaches to take over Ulsterbus and Citybus, all on an all-or-nothing basis, which would simply replace a public monopoly with a private monopoly, over which the responsible departments would have less control. In these circumstances, an employee buy-out led by managers on the same basis as bus drivers was a concept which could not easily be disregarded.

One of the key objectives of the privatisation policy was to create a degree of competition. This led to an alternative strategy being developed, in which franchises could be issued for significant areas of the Province, requiring the operator to maintain all the existing services, maintaining the principle that loss making services would be offset by cross-subsidy from more profitable routes. Local politicians would have an input into the allocation of funding and the design of the route network.

Before this could be further explored, however, the government decided upon something completely different. Ulsterbus, Citybus and Northern Ireland Railways would be brought together under the NI Transport Holding Company Board of Directors (abolishing the individual Company Boards), and a new management team, who would be 'integrated', meaning that most managers would be responsible for both bus and rail activity. To some, the proposal seemed to turn the clock back to the Ulster Transport Authority, but there was surprise that it seemed to take public transport in Northern Ireland in the opposite direction from that in Great Britain, where large units including British Rail had been subdivided, both geographically and functionally, prior to privatisation.

Although the companies retained their legal identities, the name 'Translink' was coined as a marketing name for the integrated operation; the 'link' being intended to convey to passengers the improved co-ordination they could expect in the future from their public transport services.

Translink Operations 1996–2003

Following the re-organisation of the Northern Ireland Transport Holding Company and its operating subsidiaries in 1995/6, the collective marketing name for public transport in Northern Ireland became 'TRANSLINK', although the legal framework and titles of the subsidiary companies did not change. At management level, some of the senior managers became employees of the Holding Company rather than of the subsidiaries, and there was an emphasis at this level on 'integration' of bus and train management. Overall, the heavy hand of civil servants in the Department of the Environment responsible for public transport (later shared with the Department for Regional Development) also became more evident, with severe restrictions being placed upon the re-investment of the funds generated within the businesses, and reduction in the grant aid given for new buses. Against that, some modest funding became available for specialised services for elderly and disabled potential passengers, and at a later stage, for innovative services in rural areas. These schemes reflected attention and support being given to such services in Great Britain.

Unfortunately, in the straightened circumstances of the new organisation, a call was issued for economy measures, including service reductions on bus, though not train, services. Among the early casualties of this process were some of the only recently improved Goldline services, which had not yet developed their potential patronage. Some minibus services were also cut, as they could, inevitably, be shown to be generating less revenue per vehicle than other services in the respective districts.

LINKLINE

The first evidence of 'integration', as far as public services were concerned, was the launch of 'Linkline', an attempt to promote the convenience of interchange between bus and train services. This included some co-ordination of timetables, and local signage at the selected stations such as Bangor and Newry (where a bus shuttle between the rail station and the town centre was introduced), to draw attention to the convenience of interchange. A significant draw-back was the fact that no through fares or ticketing could be offered between either bus company and Northern Ireland Railways, due to the limitations of their widely different ticketing systems. An exception, if it can be called that, was that passengers holding either bus or train tickets to or from Belfast could travel free on the *Centrelink* service, which replaced the former *Rail-Link* to and from Central Station.

Bus and rail staff promote Linkline services at Bangor.
Translink

EASIBUS

The first new services tailored specifically for passengers requiring improved access had been introduced in East Belfast in 1994. By 1997, the concept was expanded into North and South Belfast, and out to Bangor and Derry City in 1999.

RURAL BUS GRANTS

A scheme to assist the establishment of improved or innovative new bus services in rural areas was introduced in 1999. Among the twelve services launched was the restoration of the Enniskillen–Belturbet link, first introduced in 1968. This had been advertised as 'temporarily suspended' for thirty years, due to destruction of the border bridge at Aghalane. The 'Mourne Rambler' service was restored, later joined by the 'Causeway Rambler'. Other service improvements under the Rural funding included Derry–Park Bridge–Claudy; Cookstown–Pomeroy; Newtownards–Ballygowan; and Newry–Kilnasagart. A novel form of 'flexible', demand responsive service was introduced experimentally between Newcastle and Belfast. A new service for hospital patients and visitors was introduced between Bangor and the Ulster Hospital at Dundonald, and a similar service followed between Carrickfergus and Antrim Area Hospital. The Newcastle town service was recast as a rural operation.

Several of the service improvements started with Rural Bus funding have subsequently continued within the scheduled timetable.

TICKETING

Following more than a decade of using the original Wayfarer electronic ticket registers, Translink introduced the new Wayfarer TGX register into Citybus in October 2001, and into Ulsterbus in stages completing in May 2002. Although similar in size to the previous model, this system is vastly more powerful in memory and electronic functions. The unit now contains a digital version of the entire fare book required by the depot, as well as a GPS (global positioning satellite) system which enables the unit to identify its location. Once the driver has selected a journey, the unit displays the fares available from that boarding point, and automatically progresses along the fare list as each fare stage is reached. Another feature is the built in 'Smart Card' technology which enables the register to identify a Smart Card (a credit card sized item containing an embedded microchip) and react accordingly. This may vary according to the nature of the Smart Card presented. For example, the holder of a season card will be allowed to travel and the register will verify and record the journey made. This could be a card authorising a predetermined number of journeys over a section of the route, or unlimited travel within a time period or a geographical area. A Senior SmartPass identifies a passenger who is entitled to free travel under the government scheme. The register will issue a ticket to the passenger as well as recording the details and value of the journey taken, so that the bus company will be reimbursed. Another type of SmartPass will identify a passenger entitled to a discounted fare, such as half fare, permit the issue of the reduced price ticket, and record details of the journey taken and the amount of reimbursement due. Another potential use of Smart Cards is as the equivalent of a purse of money, so that as each journey is taken, the register would deduct the value of that journey from the card. The calculator within the register can also perform the driver's arithmetic, totalling a series of tickets, and displaying the amount of change due. Calculations can be switched from Sterling to Euro and back, for use on cross-border routes. The system allows much

more extensive data to be gathered than hitherto, regarding the patronage of bus services, which is used in reviewing and forward planning of bus routes and timetables. The Wayfarer TGX was also introduced to railway booking offices, and a hand-held version is carried by conductors on trains, thus giving Translink a compatible ticketing system throughout its network of operations.

BELFAST OPERATIONAL REVIEW

A very extensive study of operations in the Belfast area was undertaken between 1999 and 2001. The Greater Belfast area was examined on a corridor by corridor basis by teams of staff familiar with the operations of the routes concerned, and who studied the needs and opportunities for improvement of passenger services. Little of this work could be said to have been implemented in the immediate aftermath.

A further 'Citybus Strategic Review' led by Ted Hesketh was carried out during 2002–3. This examined the role of the operator in relation to other relevant authorities, making comparisons with Local Authorities and Public Transport Authorities in Great Britain. This clarified the distinction between 'commercial' and 'socially necessary' services and the provision of other 'overheads' such as bus stations and call centres. Further development and implementation work (which ultimately led to the Metro network) was held over until the appointment of Ted Hesketh's successor.

The March of Technology

Translink also set out to push the boundaries of technological progress for the benefit of passengers and intending passengers in other ways. A geographical information service (GIS) was introduced for service planning, drawing upon the technology within the ticketing system, and other advanced systems. The Translink system is now acknowledged within the industry to be the most advanced in the British Isles.

Real-time systems were introduced at selected busy bus stops on certain corridors in Belfast which give passengers progressive timetable information on the next buses due to reach the stop. Initially these displayed the scheduled times; increasingly the system reacts to the position of the bus, identified by the Wayfarer TGX on board, to predict the actual arrival time at succeeding stops.

Translink also introduced a web site (www.translink.co.uk) which incorporates a journey planner, allowing an intending passenger to input details of the start and end points of their journey and receive details of the most suitable route and journey times. Initially this system produced some laughable anomalies, such as an inability to distinguish between Greencastle, Co Down and Greencastle, Co Tyrone! However, the system is constantly being reviewed and upgraded, and the information is very reliable. For those wedded to more traditional communications technology, Translink also introduced a centralised call centre for all travel information (028 9066 6630).

Bus Priority

Bus priority was a field of study and development which assumed increasing importance as the decade of the 1990s progressed. The bus companies worked in close collaboration with Road Service and the other relevant authorities to generate and develop bus priority proposals and work these through to implementation.

At official levels there was increasingly a realisation that the current levels of private car usage were unsustainable, leading to worsening congestion and increasing damage to the environment. It was widely suggested that raising the quality of public transport and making it more attractive would encourage some motorists to transfer to public transport, with advantages to traffic flow as well as public transport revenues. But as bus services were already caught up in the congestion, a major part of the objective of making services more attractive depended upon easing congestion for buses compared to cars – hence the concept of priority. There were many and varied methods of progressing the objective, and whilst to say we tried, or even considered, them all during this period might be an exaggeration, this section will try to give a brief review of the progress we made.

'Bus Lanes' consist of reserving sections of the carriageway exclusively for buses. This is particularly advantageous if it allows buses to reach the stop line at a traffic light controlled junction, and get through the lights at the first 'green' phase, while non priority traffic may have to sit in a queue through two or more phases of the lights. It is a highly visible form of priority, being apparent to both bus passengers and other drivers.

The first experimental bus lanes were introduced at the approaches to four junctions on the Ormeau Road in February 1991. Three were quite short and our studies concluded that they had not been successful, but the longest lane, approaching the Ormeau Bridge, was pronounced a success, became permanent in 1992, and was extended in 1993 and 1995 to a total length of 850 metres. Whilst the 'Southern Approaches' to Belfast was a high priority route for improvement due to the lack of motorway or highway improvement available to traffic generally, it was by no means the only route on which bus priority measures were needed.

In 1990, we tabled a proposal for a major new bus service which would serve as a demonstration project for high quality public transport. This became the *City Express*, using the existing M2 motorway to bring residents of the most far flung 'suburban' areas around Belfast. However at that time the M2 ended abruptly at Nelson Street/Duncrue Street, with inevitable queues at peak times. For success, the scheme required to be seen to be able to bypass this line of traffic. The solution required a short length of 'bus only' carriageway to be built across the central reservation, together with a 400m 'contra-flow' bus lane along Nelson Street. Road Service responded with remarkable enthusiasm and alacrity to this proposal, and the bus priority route was built and ready for use in six months, allowing the new service to start in a blaze of publicity (which emphasised the benefit of bypassing the traffic queues) in May 1991.

The main thrust of bus lane development followed a period of research and observation of traffic flows. Albertbridge Road received its first bus lane (350m) in 1996; Upper Lisburn Road (400m) and Malone Road (350m) in 1997; Castlereagh Road (900m) in 1998 and Holywood Road (500m) and Crumlin Road (1500m) in 1999. Meanwhile another short 'contra flow' lane in Queens Square was provided in connection with the opening of Laganside Buscentre in 1996.

An 800m Bus lane on the Saintfield opened in 2000, contributing to development of that route as a 'Quality Corridor'. Further lanes opened on Shore Road (500m), Cregagh Road (1200m) Albertbridge Road (500m) and East Bridge Street (300m) in 2001, followed by almost 2.1km of lanes on Andersonstown Road and Falls Road in 2002.

BUSWAYS

The 'Rolls-Royce' solution to bus priority would probably be the segregated busway, which would provide a roadway or section of roadway exclusively for buses. This is not unlike the principle of railway lines, but offers several major advantages, not least that the busway can be built and used in stages, not necessarily continuous; whereas new rail lines have to be built to completion before the train service can be operated. At the end of a rail line passengers have to leave the trains and change modes if they wish to travel further, while a bus service can rejoin the roadway and continue without inconvenience. Ulsterbus was not slow to devise and promote several proposals for Busway projects. On the 'Southern Approaches', we devised the 'Super-route', countering a proposal by the government department to build a highway, which had raised massive public opposition because of its environmental impact on Belvoir Forest.

Another scheme was the 'E-way' which proposed the re-use of the former trackbed of the Comber rail line, which remains a remarkably complete potential traffic corridor between Dundonald on the eastern fringe of the City, and the inner city at Holywood Arches. This has been subjected to extensive analysis and study, and was beginning to make realistic progress toward implementation during the period of devolved government.

Another scheme was to enable buses, including longer distance express services, approaching Belfast from the west, to bypass the congestion at the city end of the M1 motorway. The scheme envisaged an additional bus lane along the M1 and Westlink and a flyover leading directly into the Europa Buscentre. After much discussion, this began to take a realistic shape when Road Service warmed to the concept of using the hard shoulder of the motorway as a peak hour bus lane. The section from Stockmans Lane to Donegall Road (1.4km) was opened in September 1999, being the first example of this technique being implemented on a motorway hard shoulder in the British Isles. An offside bus lane (400m) along Westlink to the Roden Street junction, linking in to the Busway constructed by Translink between Roden Street and Europa, opened in November 2000. The strategic importance of bus priority on this route assumed greater importance as proposals to widen the M1 motorway and construct new junctions with Westlink were announced. Indeed, extension of the bus priority measures on the motorway is expected to contribute to the measures to alleviate traffic congestion resulting from the construction work.

During 2000, the Busway from the Europa Bus Centre to the Roden Street junction on the Westlink, which links the M1 and M2 motorways, was constructed. It opened in November and allowed vehicles heading towards the M1 to reach the Westlink, avoiding the congested Grosvenor Road roundabout. Vehicles coming from the west accessed the Busway via an offside bus lane on the Westlink.
Translink

BUS STOPS

Another aspect of the operation of bus services in relation to other traffic concerns bus stops. We stressed that the design of the bus stop environment and the convenience for bus passengers of the boarding and alighting process was important to the concept of 'quality' of the bus travel experience. Very often buses were prevented from accessing the side of the road by cars parked in front of the stop. Not only did this inconvenience passengers, but also contributed to avoidable delays for other traffic.

In a major joint campaign to improve the situation, launched in 1997, Road Service introduced new red carriageway markings at bus stops, and these were supported by enhanced enforcement by police and Traffic Wardens. A Design Manual for Improved Quality of bus stop infrastructure was published jointly in the same year.

This ensured that the standards developed by the team in Belfast would spread throughout the Province.

SELECTIVE VEHICLE DETECTION

This is another technique for bus priority, in which technology at the roadside, or under the road surface, identifies the presence of a bus and influences the phasing of traffic lights at a junction ahead in its favour. Unlike the bus lane, this is 'covert' priority, not apparent to passengers or motorists, therefore having less influence over the use of cars, but being automatic, requires no enforcement. An experimental scheme was installed along the Upper Newtownards Road in 1993. The results showed that buses fitted with the activating device (known as a transponder) gained an average of one minute journey time, compared with those not fitted, though the overall effort involved in designing the project itself created further benefits to traffic flow. The scheme was not extended on a general basis, although the principle was subsequently applied to specific locations.

DROMORE BY-PASS

Bus Priority measures were not confined to those which were identified as being exclusively for buses, nor were they confined to the Belfast city area. An important achievement was the creation of an improved access for traffic from Dromore, Co Down, to the northbound carriageway of the A1 Dromore By-pass. Having identified and quantified the excessive delays suffered by bus passengers in re-joining the A1, at a junction with a history of serious and fatal accidents, fortunately not involving buses, Ulsterbus urged Roads Service to improve the

The new slip road to the Dromore By-pass was opened by Lord Dubs (right) on a blustery day in March 1998. Seen accompanying him are (left to right) John Lundy (District Manager), G Irvine Millar (Inspector General) and Jeffrey Donaldson MP.

situation. Roads Service proposed a long term study of junctions not only to the Dromore By-pass, but also to the Banbridge By-pass, and pointed out that any improvements of these junctions would require investment of millions of pounds on flyovers or underpasses at each point. In response, Ulsterbus proposed that a simple link road could be constructed from the Lurgan Road to the northbound carriageway, utilising the existing bridge to create a low cost grade separated junction. This was constructed very quickly, and opened on a wet and blustery day in March 1998, saving thousands of hours of pointless delay for Goldline passengers. Road Service did carry out their large study, which proved the need for further junction improvements, which are taking shape as this is written.

PARK AND RIDE

Another concept in which government, in the shape of Road Service, and the bus companies were able to co-operate in an effort to keep cars away from the city centre, was by providing park and ride facilities. An old established park and ride scheme in North Belfast had predated the formation of Citybus in 1973, but the facility had declined in quality, requiring the motorist to walk some distance, cross a main road, and await the next regular service bus. Due to the one-way traffic scheme the bus stops were not very convenient in either direction. This facility was re-launched as 'Northside Park and Ride' in 1995. Ulsterbus (operating through its Flexibus subsidiary) provided a dedicated midibus, departing from the parking site every fifteen minutes. Very soon, Road Service provided a new terminal slip road adjoining the parking area, giving the motorists direct access to the bus stop in both directions, without crossing the busy main roads. In 1997, a new low floor midibus was introduced, enabling the service to be promoted as fully accessible. The success of this service led to the establishment of a second, similar operation from the Eastside parking areas at Bridge Street, which commenced in 2000. Again the parking area was subsequently rebuilt, with a convenient dedicated bus terminal facility alongside.

Translink management also embraced the idea of park and ride, to encourage motorists to switch to public transport for the greater part of their journey. In many cases these comprised a re-launch or extension of existing station car parks, but the concept was applied also to bus stations, where space could be found, such as Dungannon (1998). Where possible, park and ride spaces were included in station redevelopments, several of which were joint bus and train stations, such as Bangor and Coleraine in 2001 and Antrim in 2002.

Business Review

Financial Year (to March)	Passenger Journeys (svcs)(m) Ulsterbus	Citybus	Total Revenue (£m) Ulsterbus	Citybus	Net Profit (£m) Ulsterbus	Citybus
1988–89	54.6	27.7	33.9	12.5	2.8	(0.8)
1989–90	52.4	27.9	36.5	13.9	2.3	(0.4)
1990–91	52.6	26.0	40.5	14.6	2.1	(0.4)
1991–92	51.7	25.2	44.4	15.7	2.5	0.1
1992–93	52.2	25.0	47.1	16.3	2.8	0.1
1993–94	53.4	26.2	51.0	16.8	3.7	0.5
1994–95	55.5	26.7	55.1	17.8	4.1	0.9
1995–96	55.4	25.5	57.6	17.9	3.7	0.6
1996–97	54.0	24.4	61.6	18.0	3.1	(0.1)
1997–98	51.6	23.1	63.6	17.6	4.8	(0.3)
1998–99	49.4	21.9	63.9	17.9	4.4	(0.4)
1999–00	48.2	21.3	66.1	18.6	(0.4)	(0.7)
2000–01	46.8	20.3	66.7	18.4	(6.4)	(1.7)
2001–02	44.8	18.5	69.7	19.2	(6.3)	(0.8)
2002–03	46.8	19.5	73.8	19.8	1.6	(1.2)

It is evident that Citybus patronage (measured by passenger journeys) continued to decline inexorably during the 1990s. On Ulsterbus, on the other hand the long-term declining trend was arrested and even reversed during the early 1990s, due to the success of Goldline and Busybus services in generating new business. The trend turned down again from 1995. Ironically the improving political situation in the Province resulted in reducing public transport patronage, as car owners gained confidence in using their vehicles for journeys they had previously made by public transport. This downward trend was accelerated by the service reductions imposed on bus operations by the Translink regime. Carriage of schoolchildren continued to be a major part of the Ulsterbus business. Indeed the proportion exceeded half of the total passenger journeys for the first time during the period under review.

Ulsterbus continued to generate net profits until 1999, but showed a negative figure for the next few years. Citybus, on the other hand, was able to show only very modest profits from 1991 to 1996 (its best year being 1994/5 prior to the formation of Translink) and showed increasing losses during the Translink era. Many of us would feel that these figures proved the case against the creation of Translink, which, in a sense, turned the clock back to the former Ulster Transport Authority. The organisation had once again become too large to be efficient and cost effective. Indeed senior managers have openly declared that they had to devote a disproportionate amount of their time to deal with the problems of the railways, and thereby neglected issues in bus management.

The Ulsterbus and Citybus Fleets

The Large Bus Fleet

During 1989, deliveries of Leyland Tigers with Alexander 'N' type bodies continued apace, completing chassis and body orders placed some two years earlier. This had been the Ulsterbus standard vehicle since 1983. However, behind the scenes, there were major changes happening, to understand which it is necessary to go back to 1987.

The once-mighty British Leyland Motor Corporation had been subdivided in 1987, with the Leyland Truck division passing to DAF, and the Leyland Bus division being bought by its own management team. Bus chassis were being built at the original Farington factory at Leyland, and complete vehicles in the purpose built Leyland National facility at Workington. Factories at Park Royal, Bristol, Charles Roe (Leeds, later to become Optare) and Eastern Coach Works (Lowestoft) had already been closed over the preceding years. Ulsterbus had placed a confidence boosting order for 195 Tiger chassis within a month of this re-organisation. (These were duly delivered as Ulsterbus Nos 1140–1299 with Leyland TL11 engines and air suspension, and Citybus Nos 2601–35 with Gardner engines and Taperlite single leaf suspension.)

However Leyland Bus had no direct control over manufacture of engines, and Leyland Truck had decided that continued production of the TL11 engine, particularly the horizontal version used in the Tiger coach and bus chassis, would no longer be economic. Leyland Bus offered its customers the Gardner 6HLXB or the Cummins L10 as alternative options, but installation of either of these engines required major structural alteration to the Tiger chassis side members, which did not appeal to Ulsterbus management. The Leyland TL11 engine had itself been derived from the early post war Leyland O600 unit, through the Leyland O680. DAF had also been developing from the same base engine and could offer much greater power outputs. It was known that the DAF engine could easily be fitted into the Leyland chassis. Meanwhile, Volvo, rather surprisingly, displayed a Leyland Tiger coach chassis at the 1987 Commercial Motor Show in Birmingham, to show how easily their Volvo DH10 engine could be fitted into the Tiger chassis as a service replacement unit. This horizontal engine had historically been derived from their 9.6 litre vertical engine which shared many similarities with the AEC 9.6 litre engine, as used in the Regent chassis, and had similar external dimensions to the Leyland TL11. This inspired me, and my colleague Ken Middleton, Ulsterbus Chief Engineer, to press Leyland Bus to offer the Volvo engine in the Tiger chassis.

When, a few months later in March 1988, Leyland Bus was bought over by Volvo Bus, the Ulsterbus proposal seemed assured of acceptance. For internal reasons the new management of Volvo Bus still resisted the request, but were eventually persuaded, rather than face the entire Ulsterbus order going elsewhere. At this stage, with the imminent deregulation of the bus industry in Britain, Ulsterbus/Citybus orders were among the largest bus orders available. The resultant order for 250 Leyland Tiger Chassis with Volvo engines was placed in 1988 and fulfilled by delivery from 1989 onwards of Citybus Nos 2636–2680 and Ulsterbus Nos 1300–1500 (of which Nos 1400–7 and Nos 1455–82 were delivered to Citybus). A feature of the new regime within Ulsterbus/Citybus was that Citybus were constrained to accept substantially the same specification as Ulsterbus on the Tiger chassis, rather than the very different vehicle represented by the previous batch. This, in effect, restored the group standardisation policy which had applied to deliveries of Bristol RELL chassis from 1975 to 1983.

Even then, Volvo owned Leyland Bus did not offer this version as a standard option to the home market, instead classifying it as an 'export specification' and declaring Northern Ireland as export territory. This repeated a ruse adopted previously by Leyland Bus in 1981 when agreeing to continue production of the Bristol RELL for Ulsterbus and Citybus and customers in New Zealand. The only other UK operator to receive the Volvo-engined Tiger was Lowland Scottish, to whom Ulsterbus sold four chassis, conditional upon the bodywork also being taken from the Ulsterbus production line at Alexander's Belfast factory.

The second major change was in bodywork design. Managing Director Ted Hesketh was keen to see an early change in the appearance of new buses. He sought a more modern and attractive image to replace the rather plain and functional image of the 'N' type body which Alexanders' Belfast factory had developed for Ulsterbus in 1983. He persuaded the Alexander management to bring in an external design consultant to revise the body styling. The result was the 'Q' type body, launched within the bus companies as the 'Cityliner'. Overall height of the body was raised a little, and the front and rear ends were extensively redesigned by consultant Dawson Sellars. The prototype body was built as No 1321 in 1990, and full scale production started from No 1340 for Ulsterbus and No 2636 for Citybus in 1991. Most of the Ulsterbus vehicles were 53 seaters, while those for Citybus were 51 seaters with a pram pen.

Another major business decision made by Ted Hesketh was to rebrand the network of 'Ulsterbus Express' services across the Province, including several cross border routes. This was to include a batch of new purpose built coaches, together with a new brand image and supporting network publicity material. Although Ulsterbus had purchased limited numbers of coach-bodied Leyland Leopards for such duties between 1978 and 1981 and three batches of a coach seated and specially liveried version of the standard Leyland Tiger with Alexander 'N' type body during the 1980s, the 'Ulsterbus Express' branding introduced in 1976 had become diluted by excessive application on Leyland Leopards used mainly on ordinary bus services.

Leyland Bus, although by now owned by Volvo, agreed to supply a final batch of twenty 12m Leyland Tiger coach chassis with Leyland TL11 engines and automatic transmission. These are believed to have been the last Tiger chassis assembled with TL11 engines, and were understood to constitute a cancelled MoD order. Bodywork chosen for 16 Express service coaches was the 'TE' model already supplied by Alexanders' Falkirk factory to a range of Scottish and English operators, and indeed to Bus Éireann, but the Ulsterbus vehicles were assembled in the Belfast factory, and delivered in 1990, in the striking new 'Goldliner' livery, also designed by Dawson Sellars. The remaining four of the 20 chassis were allocated to Duple Coachbuilders at Blackpool to receive their 340 style luxury coach bodywork for the Ulsterbus Tours fleet, although the first of these was almost immediately transferred to the Express service fleet to launch the new Belfast to Dublin service, to which the Department had finally granted an operating licence after years of asking. These were the last coach bodies purchased from Duple, as that company closed soon afterwards.

The 'Goldline Express' concept was immediately successful; to such an extent that another batch of service coaches was urgently required. The first batch of the new 'Q' type bodies, although on 11m chassis, was hurriedly re-specified as Goldliner (Mark II) coaches with 49 reclining seats, for delivery in 1991, and used to extend the Goldline concept and livery to include a number of routes which had had to be omitted from the allocation of the first batch.

In 1990, Volvo made it clear that production of the Leyland Tiger would cease after completion of the current order, and the search for a suitable replacement resumed, especially for city services, for which adoption of the Leyland Tiger had only been an interim expedient. At this stage, much attention was being given throughout the bus industry to ease of access. The need for lower steps and flat floors was widely recognised, but manufacturers had not yet introduced ultra low floor designs to the British market, although such designs were available on the continent.

In 1990, the Tours Department took delivery of four new coaches on DAF MB230 chassis with the contemporary Plaxton Paramount body. The decision to buy DAF chassis was surprising, as the company had experience of only one example of that make, acquired with the business of Sureline Coaches in 1987, There is little doubt that the decision to buy these DAFs was a tactic in the company's negotiations with Volvo, to demonstrate its preparedness to switch major orders to a new supplier if it was not satisfied with the alternatives on offer. Around the time the decision was being taken to order new DAFs, six second-hand coaches of that make were also acquired. The new DAF/Plaxton coaches were followed by five more similar coaches in 1991, and a further two in 1993.

Meanwhile, production of the Volvo-engined Tiger chassis with Alexanders 'Q' type bodies for the service bus fleet continued through 1991/2. A significant decision taken during this period was to purchase a trial batch of chassis to the full 12m permissible length. Although well established for touring and express service coaches, there had been reservations about the use of this size of vehicle on local Ulsterbus routes. The longer dimension permitted seating capacity to be increased to 64, with seats for 3 and 2 on either side of the gangway. This made a major contribution to providing additional seating capacity at peak times for the carriage of schoolchildren, which continued to be a major part of the Ulsterbus business. The first 12m vehicles to arrive were eight coaches for Citybus, to take over the successful new *City Express* service; these had 53 luxury coach seats. A further batch of 25 standard length vehicles for Citybus (Nos 1455–79) had dual purpose seating, as fitted to most of the Ulsterbus vehicles and these were followed by a further three which, although only 11m in length, were equipped as 49 seat coaches to supplement the *City Express* fleet.

Another batch of 20 Goldliner coaches was taken into stock in 1992, ordered soon after the Mark II batch, which had only been regarded as a short term measure. These were 12m Leyland Tigers (Volvo-engined) and were fitted with 'Endeavour' coach style bodies by Wrights of Ballymena, which became known as the Mark III Goldliners. This was, significantly, the first quantity order for full-size bodies placed by Ulsterbus with Wrights.

The final Leyland Tiger entered service in 1993. A total of 784 new buses and coaches of this marque had been purchased for the Ulsterbus and Citybus fleets (plus 13 pre-owned coaches) – almost certainly the largest fleet of this type anywhere in the world, and exceeding the impressive totals of 685 Leyland Leopards and 620 Bristol RELLs purchased between 1967 and 1983; with the greater number of second-hand vehicles, the grand totals of each of these latter types operated actually exceeded the total of Leyland Tigers.

However the search for a more suitable chassis for urban services was still in progress. An extensive research programme included testing a range of demonstration vehicles of various rear-engined models in Citybus service, mainly on the Dundonald services.

The companies next placed an order for a quantity of Dennis Dart buses with 39-seat Wrights 'Handybus' bodywork. Both shorter and narrower than contemporary buses, these were considered suitable for a range of lighter rural services and for some urban services where the operation of full-size single-

The last Tiger to enter service was No 1500, which was allocated to Lisburn. It is seen here well away from the Sprucefield route, at Blackpool Transport's Rigby Road depot in 1998 when it been in attendance at a bus rally at Leyland, Lancs. The tiger's head badge was specially fitted for the occasion.
Paul Savage

deckers might no longer be justified. A few were even earmarked to boost capacity on *Busybus* services on which demand had exceeded the capacity available with the standard Mercedes midibus. The batch was split between Ulsterbus and Citybus, and was delivered in 1994. One Citybus vehicle (No 624) received a modified specification to equip it for a new type of service specially designed for the elderly and disabled passengers who might otherwise have been unable or reluctant to use public transport, and which was to be supported by new funding from the Department of the Environment under the brand name *Easibus*. This vehicle had only 34 seats and included a wheelchair lift.

In the same year, Citybus received the first two articulated coaches ever purchased for service in Ireland. These Volvo B10MA-55 chassis had Van Hool Alizee bodywork which, although built to an urban service specification, featured luxury coach seating. These were intended to provide additional capacity on the popular *City Express* service and to make a striking public image statement.

By this time, Volvo Bus management had finally persuaded Ulsterbus to accept the Volvo B10M as replacement chassis for the Tiger, for inter-urban and rural services. Fifty of these started to come through in 1994, with Alexander 'Q' type 65-seat bodies. There were also fifty with Plaxton Premier coach bodies destined for Goldline Express service, and designated Mark IV Goldliners, the first Goldliners with 'full luxury' bodies from a traditional coach (as distinct from bus) builder. Such a large order might have been expected to displace some of the earlier Goldliners from this type of service. However, such was the expansion of the business that there was still no concerted cascading of the early vehicles. Indeed the Mark I vehicles were thoroughly refurbished for continued Goldline service.

The Tours Department also reverted to the company standard chassis choice, taking Volvo B10M chassis with the superior Plaxton Excalibur coachwork, two being delivered in 1994 and five in 1995.

Vehicles delivered in 1996 comprised the last orders placed by Ulsterbus/Citybus before the change of management structure associated with the formation of Translink. The bulk of this order comprised repeat orders for standard models. A batch of 30 Volvo B10M chassis with Plaxton Premier bodies brought the Goldliner Mark IV fleet up to 80 coaches, yet still the Mark I, II and III Goldliners were needed for Goldline service at least at peak times.

With the advent of the ultra-low floor concept for ease of access, Ulsterbus/Citybus were anxious to maximise the input of this type of vehicle for city services. After reviewing several models the order was placed with Alexanders who were collaborating with Volvo to produce the 'Ultra' body, assembled in the Belfast factory, on the Volvo B10L under-frame. The order was for 60 vehicles, later augmented with two of the pre-production prototypes, one of which had served as a demonstrator with Citybus. As these were city service buses, they were intended primarily for Citybus, but ten were allocated to Ulsterbus for city services in Derry.

As the two Volvo B10MA/Van Hool Alizee articulated coaches bought in 1994 for Citybus had operated successfully – indeed one had also proved its worth on Ulsterbus Goldline Services – a further two were purchased in 1996 for Goldline Express operation. These had the more luxurious coach specification, with higher floor level, fewer but more comfortable reclining seats, and substantial luggage capacity.

In the same year the Tours Department received six more luxury coaches on Volvo B10M chassis. The first two, built to the short 9m length, had Caetano Algarve II bodies, a first order for this manufacturer, while the remaining four had Plaxton Excalibur bodies similar to those already operating.

After the reorganisation of public transport which created Translink in 1996, the rules imposed by the government departments concerned for investment by the Transport Holding Company changed dramatically. For more than two decades Ulsterbus had successfully operated a simple system whereby funds generated within the business each year were invested in new buses the following year. The Government had reimbursed a proportion of the funding in New Bus Grants after 1974, and the Monopolies and Mergers Commission in 1989 had confirmed that although such grants had ceased in Great Britain, this form of government assistance, in the absence of route or network subsidies, remained appropriate for the Northern Ireland situation.

However, Government had now invented the Private Finance Initiative. Translink was forbidden to invest its funds in new buses and were directed to seek private finance for fleet renewal. As the rest of the British bus industry had been privatised there was no other public sector demand for private finance for buses and the bus manufacturers were not interested in pursuing the concept for such a limited sector of their market. Within Translink, reserves accumulated which could not be used. Even the responsible direct rule minister, Lord Alf Dubs, was sympathetic but powerless in the face of Treasury instructions. Then the unforgivable happened. The Chancellor of the Exchequer, Gordon Brown, visited the Province to announce a new spending initiative, based on funds expected to come from privatisations within Northern Ireland. However, the anticipated funding sources did not materialise and, instead, civil servants 'confiscated' some £25 million of accumulated reserves from the Transport Holding Company and diverted these to projects unconnected with public transport.

Eventually, common sense did prevail and the insistence on private finance was dropped, but not before lasting damage had been done to the fleet age profile, with more than three years passing without fleet renewal.

Limited approval for purchase of new vehicles was at last obtained to allow orders to be placed for delivery in 1999/2000. These included 30 Volvo B10M coaches for Goldline Express services, differing from previous purchases in having the more luxurious Plaxton Excalibur bodies. Ten of these had toilets and other luxury features, while specification of the others followed previous practice. These became known as the Mark V and Mark VI Goldliners and their arrival did at last allow the older Mark II coaches to be downgraded to bus duties. The Tours Department also benefited from four Volvo B10M/Plaxton Excalibur coaches similar to previous orders, while two of the Mark VI Goldliners were actually allocated to the same department and dedicated to the mainland operation of the Ulsterbus cross-channel express services, in Eurolines livery.

Continued advances in the design of low floor buses had resulted in the discontinuance of the Volvo B10L/Alexander 'Ultra' combination and Translink opted for the Volvo B10BLE with Wrights Renown bodywork, with which Robert Wright and Son were already achieving impressive sales throughout the

New low floor buses purchased for delivery in 2001 were 38 Scania L94UBs with Wright Solar bodies. All were allocated, initially, to Ulsterbus depots. No 710 is seen in Royal Avenue, Belfast in August 2002 in original condition with the contrasting coloured swoops and faired-in rear wheelarches.

Paul Savage

British Isles. An order for 90 of these was initially divided equally between Citybus and Ulsterbus, and the completed vehicles were delivered in 1999 and 2000. In order to test another type of low floor urban bus, an order was also placed with Mercedes-Benz for ten integral single-deckers, of which four were to be articulated buses. All ten were delivered in 2000 and specified for the *City Express* service, However the standard of the seating fitted proved very disappointing for this high profile service, and the vehicles were more widely used on regular Citybus routes.

One Scania L94UB with Wright Solar body was received in 2000, initially as a demonstrator, but subsequently purchased. This was to be the precursor for a further change in policy when 38 Scania L94UBs with Wright Solar bodies were purchased for delivery during 2001.

In the same year, Citybus took delivery of a batch of Volvo B7TL double-deck buses with Alexander ALX400 76-seat bodies. These were remarkable in being the first new double-deckers purchased by either company since 1974, and indicated a major shift in policy. Several were destined for use on Quality Corridor services under the 'Go' branding, while others took over operation of the *City Express* service from the Mercedes previously mentioned. Two went to Ulsterbus for the *Unilink* service, which had started as a minibus route only ten years earlier!

The Tours Department were able to purchase five Volvo B10M coaches with Caetano Enigma bodies in 2001, but these may prove to be the last Volvo B10Ms purchased, as the order for 2002 delivery was placed with Scania for the K114 chassis, mounted with Irizar Century bodies.

Double-deckers, in the shape of Alexander ALX 400-bodied Volvo B7TLs, returned to the streets of Belfast in 2001. *Translink*

By the end of 2002, with the average age of the group fleets far higher than at any time since the early 1970s, it seemed that at last some sensible attention was being given to fleet renewal, with orders for delivery during 2003–4 being placed for 35 Optare Solos for the *Busybus* fleet, 25 Volvo B7TL / Alexander ALX400 double-deckers (mainly for Citybus), 80 Scania L94UB/Wrightbus Solar single-deckers (mainly for Ulsterbus), and 50 new Goldliner coaches, for which the choice of Scania K94IB chassis and Irizar InterCentury bodies marked another major change of practice.

Further orders were expected to follow authorisation of £40 million funding for 300 new buses over three years. However these orders were not confirmed within the period covered by this volume, with the result that the average age of the fleet continued to rise, reaching a higher level than at any time since the formation of Ulsterbus and Citybus from their predecessor organisations (1967 and 1973). At this stage, there were still large numbers of Bristol RELL and Leyland Leopard buses well over 20 years old, while even the early deliveries of Leyland Tiger buses had almost reached that age. This was altogether a major collapse of the policy of replacing buses at around sixteen years of age, which had been resolutely maintained by Ulsterbus/ Citybus for more than thirty years from the formation of Ulsterbus in 1967 until the creation of Translink in 1996.

The Small Bus Fleet

The 'Flexibus' branding, which covered small buses used on contract and private hire, had been started in 1984 and had expanded to almost 40 buses, most of which were van conversions from the Ulsterbus workshops. At the start of the period covered by this volume, the last of these conversions were taking shape in the form of four Mercedes 811Ds with 19 coach seats.

The *Busybus* concept – minibus town services in provincial towns – had already been launched late in 1987 and was proving successful in expanding Ulsterbus passenger patronage. Although the business had been started with vehicles converted from panel vans in Ulsterbus' own workshops, it had become apparent that a slightly larger vehicle with purpose-built bodywork would give more capacity and flexibility in operation, and hopefully a more durable service life, akin to full-size buses. An order had been placed for 40 such buses on Mercedes-Benz 709D chassis cowls and with Wright 'TS' bodies, to be delivered during 1989. This was the first large order placed by Ulsterbus with the Ballymena coachbuilder, at a time when they were rapidly expanding their sales and customer range throughout the British Isles.

Small buses (MCW Metroriders) had been introduced on the *Airbus* service in 1988. As vehicles on this service achieved very high annual mileages, and the company were determined to maintain a high quality standard on this flagship operation, the policy evolved that new *Airbus* vehicles should be introduced every two to three years, allowing the previous batch to be cascaded down to less demanding duties, usually in the Flexibus fleet. Thus, a further batch of five Mercedes 811D chassis with Wright 'TS' bodies was purchased in 1990 specifically for the *Airbus* service. These were slightly longer than the *Busybus* vehicles, to allow for installation of internal luggage racks, without significantly reducing seating capacity. The Wrights bodywork also featured a revised front end called the 'fast front', replacing the original Mercedes cowl, although retaining the original windscreen glass. These vehicles also featured underslung wheelchair lifts mounted towards the rear of the near side, enabling the company to promote wheelchair accessibility on this high profile service. This was a precursor of the trend which was sweeping the bus industry at the time, and which would soon result in the development of ultra low floor buses which allow passengers in wheelchairs to board and alight through the normal service doorway.

A second batch of 20 Wright 'TS'-bodied Mercedes 'Busybuses' was delivered in 1991, and a third batch of 10 in 1993, together with a second group of four for the *Airbus* service, although not with the under slung wheelchair lift. All these vehicles continued to feature the 'fast front' styling.

An unusual single vehicle purchased in 1995 was No 1814, the Mercedes 811D with Wright 'TS' body designed and built specially for the *Causeway Coaster* shuttle service at the Giant's Causeway, for which Ulsterbus had taken over responsibility from the National Trust. Although outwardly similar to the Mercedes/Wright 'TS' vehicles already purchased for the *Airbus* service, this vehicle featured a new and unusual solution to the wheelchair accessibility requirement, which I designed. Behind the rear axle, the body featured a low full width platform with a separate manual entrance door. There were also steps down from the gangway which allowed the platform to double as a standing area. Although portable wheelchair ramps are required, this layout greatly facilitated access for wheelchair passengers. Inspiration for the design came from recollection of the ease of entry and low platform height achieved on rear entrance double-deckers in years past. The following year another special vehicle was created for the *Causeway Coaster* service by modification of one of the cascaded *Airbus* Mercedes, No 1813, to offer a 'Paris-style' open air rear platform where passengers could enjoy the full effect of the summer breezes prevalent at Ulster's most popular tourist spot. Clear plastic curtains were fitted to give protection against inclement weather. In practice, the vehicle was rarely used in its 'open air' format.

The Flexibus subsidiary company also purchased five new Renault Master minibuses, with Oughtred and Harrison-converted bodies, for its educational service contracts in 1995.

The Giant's Causeway, on the North Antrim coast, is one of the Province's major tourist attractions. A shuttle service is operated to the Causeway from the visitors centre using specially-modified Mercedes 811Ds Nos 1814 (right) and 1813 (below).
John Goan (right)/ Translink (below)

By 1996, Alexanders had concentrated all midibus production in the Belfast factory, while Wrights, having secured a major share of the British market, were now very heavily committed with full-size buses. No manufacturer was yet offering a well-proven low floor small bus, so it was not surprising that the next batch for *Busybus* services were similar to what had gone before, and comprised a batch of 30 on Mercedes 711D chassis, although bodied by Alexander. This batch allowed for further expansion of the operation as well as the replacement of many of the earlier, van-based, vehicles.

Continuing the policy of replacing the *Airbus* service vehicles every two or three years, four Optare Metroriders were bought in 1996, the first order secured by Optare for Northern Ireland.

A real oddity appearing in the fleet in 1996 was the Gentrac 'road train' comprising a tractor, 'dressed up' as a steam locomotive and hauling a train of three trailers, one of which was wheelchair accessible. This was similar to the 'tourist trains' operated in many European countries, and was used to provide a summer seasonal tourist route around Portrush.

The only vehicles taken in during 1997 were two Dennis Dart SLF midibuses with Wright Crusader bodies, intended for expansion of the *Easibus* service concept in Citybus, and funded by the Department. A further batch of three Wright Crusader low floor midibuses on Dennis Dart SLF chassis was purchased in 1999, again with special funding from the Department for Regional Development to expand the range of easy access services introduced under the *Easibus* branding both in Citybus and Ulsterbus territory.

Right: Gentrac road train No 2900 joined the Ulsterbus fleet in 1996 for use on a summer season service around the North Coast resort of Portrush. It is seen here at the launch with Ted Hesketh and local councillors in attendance.   *Translink*

Below: Dart No 645 at the specially-designed terminal at Northside Park and Ride, York Street, Belfast.
Author

Another small batch of three shorter Wright Crusaders on Dennis Dart SLF low floor midibuses had also been ordered, as replacements for *Busybus* vehicles recently destroyed, and these were delivered in 1999. However, on delivery, the low floor characteristics resulted in all three being used for new shuttle services in the Belfast area.

In 2000, a batch of ten Optare Solo midibuses was delivered. These were funded by the Department under a new Rural Transport Fund, and were used largely to create new services in rural areas of the Province. However, they were also significant in representing the first successful low floor design in this category of bus, and this model was destined to later become the standard for *Busybus* replacement. Another activity of the Rural Transport Fund has been the funding of a fleet of minibuses, which, although owned and maintained by Ulsterbus, are operated by local community groups throughout the rural districts. Under this scheme a total of 14 Renault Master minibuses were delivered in 1999/2000, six Mercedes 410D Sprinters in 1999 and five Mercedes 413cDi in 2001, all with Nu-Track body conversions.

In the same year, another batch of four Dennis Dart SLF midibuses with Wright Crusader bodywork was purchased to take over the *Airbus* service. These 25-seat vehicles, with dual purpose seating, continued the tradition of having large internal luggage racks for passengers' luggage.

In 2002, the Flexibus subsidiary company, having survived throughout the 1990s on second-hand coaches, was able to purchase its first new vehicles since 1989 (other than the specialised Renault minibuses in 1995). Four Mercedes 814D with Plaxton Cheetah 24-seat luxury coach bodies were followed by nine Optare Solo 24/25-seat buses, some of which are dedicated to the company's *Airlink* service to and from Belfast City Airport.

The Search For New Identities

One of the small management groups set up by Ted Hesketh in 1989 was charged with reviewing the corporate identities, and livery presentations. At first this group interpreted their brief as requiring an entirely new livery proposal. The result was very different from past practice, using a much darker blue for Ulsterbus and a darker red for Citybus, coupled with white diagonal panels on each side and over most of the roof. The whole effect was set off with gold lining. However this proposal did not find ready acceptance, not least because of the huge cost and time delay involved to carry out a total repaint of the entire fleet.

Ulsterbus Leyland Tiger No 409 and Citybus Bristol RE No 2171 were repainted to display these proposals. Neither vehicle entered service in these paint schemes.

Raymond Bell (upper)/Paul Savage (lower)

It soon became apparent that although there was a desire to freshen up the appearance of the fleet, a totally new livery was not required. In the meantime an external consultant had been briefed by Alexanders coachworks in connection with the body styling, who, as part of his overall design, included a livery proposal based on an updating of the existing Ulsterbus scheme. The main feature was a strong line of the blue along the cantrail, curving down at the rear and continuing along the bodyside panels just above the existing blue of the lower panels. This attractive scheme was readily accepted as a basis for the new vehicles and the brief for the committee was simplified to determining how a similar effect could be achieved on existing vehicle types with the least implications on cost and time. The final results included subtle changes in the shades of blue and red (the new blue was that already adopted some years earlier on luxury coaches), and retention of the ivory as base colour for buses, which allowed the use of white to continue on coaches and other special liveries.

One feature adopted to assist passengers, was a decision to use the main fleet blue or red around the destination display on the front of the vehicle, to assist identification of the operator of the vehicle as it approached the bus stop, especially in heavy traffic when the lower part of the front end might be obstructed from view. This policy had been adopted in the livery designed for the N type Tiger body, but had not been applied retrospectively. The overall effect of the N type livery was felt to be too dark, so the new livery for that type, whilst retaining the dark colour

Leyland Tiger No 371 (left) and Leyland Leopard No 236 (below) display versions of the revised schemes, based on that being proposed by the consulatant reviewing Alexanders body designs. Neither represents the final version agreed for retrospective application.
Raymond Bell (both)

over the front dome, reverted to the use of the light ivory for most of the roof. On this type of vehicle the blue (or red) band along the cantrail was introduced, together with the downsweep at the rear, but this terminated at the existing lower colour panel rather than running along the bodyside. On the older buses (Leyland Leopards and Bristol RELLs) the blue line was not adopted, the main change noticeable on these being the introduction of the blue around the destination panel, neatly fitted into the moulded shape of the dome. Thus the cost of introducing the changes was minimised, especially on the older types of buses.

The other area of significant development was a search for revised lettering to be used both on vehicle liveries and other publicity applications. The decision was made in principle to retain the logo which was now widely recognised as representing Ulsterbus, although it had been interpreted and applied in widely different forms. The logo was redrawn with bolder, more confident lines, and it was determined that a high degree of control and standardisation should be imposed upon its many applications.

A publicity agency had introduced the use of the Roden letterface, and suggested it be adopted throughout the companies. However it soon became clear that this was not universally suitable, and indeed the need for different lettering styles for different branded products was soon seen to be justified. The Roden letterface was adopted for the Ulsterbus Tours Department, and other aspects of its operations including the cross-channel express service network. It was also adopted for the Airbus service at that time, and remained in use over several fleet renewals.

However another, quite distinctive, presentation of the basic fleetnames was designed to be used in conjunction with the new livery for service buses. This consisted of the names in italic capitals with small triangular serifs to the rear of appropriate letters, giving a 'go faster' effect. The whole name stood out from a rectangle of the livery colour, but was standing upon the colour band which formed part of the livery. The names were applied to the vehicles on the cantrail level (as had been adopted on N type bodies) whilst the previous practice of applying fleetnames on the waistrail of older body types was discontinued. However the new version of the logo, which still depended for optimum effect upon being displayed against a light background, was moved below the waistline to be displayed on the panel above the wheel arch, a location which, unlike other body panels, was seldom invaded for other purposes such as commercial or service advertising. A version of the logo was produced for display against a dark background, but was rarely adopted.

Another lettering style (Gillies Gothic) was adopted for the Goldline project, and applied both to vehicles and other publicity. This style was also used to create the Ulsterbus Coach Hire branding on luxury coaches allocated to provincial depots (and the driving school). The existing styles adopted on Busybus and Flexibus brands were retained.

A few years after the formation of Translink, the search for a new livery started all over again. On this occasion, external consultants were employed to prepare proposals, based upon the green shades which had been chosen to be the Translink corporate colour. The result was a livery on which sea green and mint green predominated, but with small areas of blue, or red being retained to enable passengers to identify the operators (though sadly not at a distance in heavy approaching traffic!). The consultants seemed unaware that this livery was strongly reminiscent of the pale scheme employed by the erstwhile Ulster Transport Authority. This livery was to be applied only on low floor buses, which meant that there would be little need to apply the new scheme retrospectively, as only the Volvo B10L/Alexander 'Ultra' buses fell into this group. The small batch of Mercedes O405 buses delivered in 2000 appeared in the previous livery, as the manufacturer had already painted the body shells before the new specification was notified.

Tiger No 519 in the first version of Goldline livery, which was not adopted.
Raymond Bell

Translink logo. The word 'company' was later replaced with 'service'.
Norman Johnston

On repaints of older buses, the opportunity was soon taken to simplify the livery application, by omitting some of the stripes, in the interests of economy. After a few years even the curved sweeps of colour on the new livery, which had helped to disguise the cubist shape of the modern bus, was deleted for the same reason.

Ulsterbus Volvo B10L/Alexander Ultra No 2759 was painted, experimentally, into this light-colured scheme; Citybus No 2749 was similarly painted with red replacing the blue. The scheme wasn't adopted but a revised version, with the darker green predominant to the rear of the entrance door, was.
Author

Special Events

Over the years the company has held a number of 'Family Fun Days' for its staff, as a way of saying "Thank You" for all of the effort that has been put into maintaining and developing operations.

Major public events, such as Belfast's Lord Mayor's Show, have been supported, too, but perhaps the Citybus-sponsored Balloon Carnivals, held in 1992 and 1993, were the most high profile.

Left: At the 1989 Family Fun Day, recently-retired Bristol LH No 1629, new in 1973, was handed to the Irish Transport Trust for preservation.
Translink

Right: The Citybus-sponsored balloon is seen here at the 1992 event in Botanic Gardens. One of the Leyland Tigers specially painted to promote the event can be glimpsed in the background.
Translink

33

The Fleet in 1988

After several livery experiments, described on page 30 , it was decided in 1989 that the older buses in the fleet would continue to bear similar liveries, with slight changes in shade of blue and red, and with new fleetnames and a refurbished version of the well-established logo. Further livery changes were introduced from 1997, following the formation of Translink, although on the older vehicles these were quite minor.

Bristol REs and Leyland Leopards were to see the least change in their established livery. No 2318 was photographed in Pennyburn depot, Londonderry in 1996 soon after being transferred from Citybus to Ulsterbus. Alongside it, No 2313, also transferred from the Citybus fleet, had already been repainted.

Author

By 1993, there were very few vehicles remaining in the pre-1989 livery. Leyland Leopard No 176 was photographed in September of that year outside Enniskillen depot, the older style logos contrasting with Leyland Leopard No 149 parked behind. *John Goan*

Leyland Leopard No 272 displays the new livery to good effect at the Islandmagee terminus of service 169, in October 1993. The driver is Sam Wylie. The background is occupied by the cross-channel ferries *Pride of Ailsa* (P&O), operating to Cairnryan, and *Stena Caledonia* (Stena Sealink), operating to Stranraer from Larne Harbour. Later the Stena service was transferred to Belfast. *Paul Savage*

Numerically the last of the 600 Bristol RELLs to be bought by Ulsterbus/ Citybus between 1975 and 1983, No 2600, normally based in Ballycastle, was on this occasion pictured in Bangor taking part in the 1993 Bus and Coach Rally. Unfortunately, No 2600 was maliciously destroyed in 1996. *Richard Whitford*

Having been chosen to represent the Ulsterbus fleet on the front cover of 'Buses in Ulster' Vol 4, Bristol RELL No 2441 was 'dressed up' in the original Ulsterbus fleetname transfers to act as a background for publicity photographs at the launch of that book in 2002. At that time the bus had been withdrawn and held in reserve, but surprisingly it returned to service soon after the book launch, still wearing the historic fleetnames, and was captured by the camera in August 2002 at Rosevale Park. *Paul Savage*

Centre exit Bristol REs were still much in evidence in 1989, but were being progressively reduced in numbers by 1996 when this shot of No 2345 was taken at Donegall Square East. No 2345 was working on the Lisburn Road service to Dunmurry and Conway Estate.
Raymond Bell

Citybus Bristol RE No 2562 still displays the revised livery and fleetnames in this shot taken at Dundonald terminus in December 1997. However, the poster at the rear indicates that the Translink name and logo were already in use by that time but had not yet been applied to all the buses.
John Goan

As there were similar vehicles in both fleets, it was not unusual for Bristol REs to be loaned between companies when a vehicle shortage arose. On this occasion, in April 1993, Citybus No 2336 was leaving Europa Buscentre on the Ulsterbus service to Twinbrook, the liberal use of paper bills being a genuine attempt to avoid confusing potential passengers.
Raymond Bell

37

Bristol RELL No 2568, photographed at Twinbrook, Lisburn in October 2003, displays the revised fleetname and logo introduced by the Translink regime. No 2568 had been transferred from Citybus to Ulsterbus in May 2000. Note the Buspak advertising boards.
Paul Savage

Leyland Leopard No 129, of 1978 vintage, was still working hard when this shot was taken in September 2000 in Scotch Street, Dungannon, as it heads out to Aughnacloy on service 76. It's wearing Translink logos.
John Goan

Fleet number 109 was re-registered while out of use in 1998, in anticipation of disposal. However the bus was re-instated and remained in service until 2006, by then the oldest example of the type in regular use, and even had to be re-numbered 4109 on arrival of a new coach to which the number 109 had been allocated. The photograph was taken in Dungannon depot in April 2001.
Richard Whitford

1989 was a year in which Ulsterbus was able to withdraw many vehicles representing the clearance of the residue of batches purchased during the mid-1970s. Included were Bedford YRQs and YLQs, pre-1974 Leyland Leopards and Daimler Fleetlines, as well as second-hand acquisitions from the 1980s.

Bedford YRQ No 1764 was spotted crossing the Newry River in Newry in March 1989. It was withdrawn, together with all remaining buses of that type, later in the same year.
Paul Savage

Also photographed in March 1989 was Bedford YLQ No 1867, in Armagh, where the Mall was still in use as the principal terminal. This bus was also withdrawn, with most of the type, in the same year, although two survived until 1990. In the background Bus Éireann Bombardier KE 26 (originally a CIÉ Tours International luxury coach) is making the Dublin connection with the Coleraine–Armagh service, operated for many years by No 538, one of the two 11m Leyland Tigers with Wright 'Contour' bodywork.
Paul Savage

Two of the Leyland Atlanteans which had been bought from Lothian Regional Transport in 1985/6 were photographed in Omagh bus station in March 1989. Both vehicles, Nos 995 and 996, were withdrawn later that year.
John Goan

By 1989, few of the Daimler Fleetlines, purchased by Belfast Corporation and Citybus up to 1973, remained in service. No 2865 was photographed in February of that year in front of Parliament Buildings, Stormont, while operating a 'Farewell Tour' for members of the Irish Transport Trust.
Paul Savage

40

Daimler Fleetline No 2863 was a survivor, however. Having been rebodied after serious fire damage in 1974, it was chosen for conversion to open-top layout in May 1991 and in that guise continued to give useful service in the Citybus Tours and Private Hire fleet until 2002. This photograph, taken outside Queens University in August 1994, displays the first version of the multicoloured stripe livery applied to the Citybus Tours fleet.   *Raymond Bell*

Another picture of No 2863 illustrates the second version of the multi-coloured stripe livery, applied with a skirt of Citybus red. It was taken in Royal Avenue, one of the city's main shopping thoroughfares, and noted for some fine 'art deco' period architecture.   *Paul Savage*

Another Daimler which survived the general withdrawal of that type was No 2857. This had already been set aside for use as the Citybus Tours bus since 1986. By 1991 it had lost its original livery of white with bold red stripes and was operating in a restrained allover white livery. It is seen at the Garmoyle Street entrance to Belfast Harbour during the 'Tall Ships' event in June 1991.

Author

In 1995, Daimler Fleetline No 2857 was thoroughly restored to its original condition and livery as delivered to Citybus in 1973 (excepting only the fact that it had been rebodied in 1976 with a body of the slightly later style fitted to the Leyland Atlanteans delivered in 1974). It was then presented to the Ulster Folk and Transport Museum in Cultra, where it is seen outside the Transport Gallery, in which it is now exhibited.

Ian Houston

This ex-Sureline Bedford YMT/Plaxton Supreme, No 690, was adopted by the Ulsterbus Driving School in 1989 (and photographed after being lettered for the purpose) and remained on training duties until 1995. *Paul Savage*

Few of the coaches acquired with the business of Sureline Coaches of Lurgan in June 1987 survived beyond 1989, mainly due to the non-standard nature of the coach fleet. The buses, of course, had already been withdrawn once by Ulsterbus before being acquired by Sureline, and were withdrawn again almost immediately after the takeover. This Ford R1114 with Duple Dominant coachwork had become No 694 in the Ulsterbus fleet and was photographed in Lisburn depot in June 1989. It was withdrawn later in the same year. *Paul Savage*

The flagship of the Sureline fleet had been this DAF MB200DKTL with Plaxton Viewmaster body, which became Ulsterbus No 697. Although hurriedly given a unique version of the Ulsterbus coach livery in 1987, it had been repainted into the full, standard, coach livery by the time this picture was taken during an enthusiasts' tour visiting the Pennyburn premises of the Lough Swilly bus operations, in 1990. Later it also was taken into the training fleet and underwent another livery change, before being withdrawn in 1999.
Paul Savage

43

Two of these Leyland Leopard/Plaxton coaches were transferred from Ulsterbus to Citybus in 1989 to form the mainstay of that company's private hire fleet. No 561 was photographed in June of that year in front of Belfast's City Hall, in its first livery, which was simply its original Ulsterbus livery with the blue stripes painted red. *Paul Savage*

Later these stripes were replaced by a simpler style of two red diagonal stripes. When the vehicles were transferred back to Ulsterbus, these stripes were repainted blue, and the coaches remained in service in that unusual livery until withdrawal. As this photograph of No 561, taken in Aughnacloy in December 1996, clearly shows, white panelling is not a suitable livery for buses on local service during the winter months! *John Goan*

Leyland Leopard/Duple Dominant II No 1995 departs from Great Victoria Street bus station in May 1990, during the construction of Europa Buscentre. By this time these coaches had been relegated to express service duties, and the fleetnames no longer included the word 'Tours'. *Paul Savage*

Similar coach No 1992 is shown in August 1991 in Magherafelt, by now displaying the new Ulsterbus fleetnames. Interestingly, due to the limited space available on the side panelling, the logo has been omitted, and replaced by the fleetname normally displayed above the cantrail. *Author*

No 551, one of the four Duple Caribbean coaches from 1983, acquired a Carribean II front end after suffering accident damage. When this picture was taken in May 1995 it still displayed the original 'Ulsterbus Tours' livery introduced on those coaches, with the later addition of dark blue skirts, but it had gained the 'Ulsterbus Coach Hire' lettering signifying coaches allocated to provincial depots primarily for private hire.

Richard Whitford

Volvo B9M/Plaxton Paramount coach No 600, purchased in 1986, remained on the strength of the Tours fleet for several years, and is seen with the revised 'Ulsterbus Tours' lettering in September 1996.

Ian Houston

Two batches of trial vehicles had been taken into the fleet during the search for an acceptable replacement for the Bristol RELL – the Leyland B21s in 1981 and the Leyland Lynxes in 1986. It was soon apparent that neither type would be purchased in quantity and by 1991 the fleet position was such that these nonstandard groups of vehicles could be sold.

The first prototype B21 became Ulsterbus No 3000 and was the only one of the batch built with a centre exit door. The livery also differed, in having the blue over the whole roof. In this photograph taken at the 1990 bus rally, at Carrickfergus, the vehicle is still displaying the old style fleetname.
Richard Whitford

Leyland B21 No 3005 was transferred from Ulsterbus to Citybus in July 1989. Surprisingly, it was painted in this RE-style livery, non-standard for Citybus B21s (cf 'Buses in Ulster' Vol 5, p118). It was sold, with the rest of the batch, to Ipswich Buses in 1991.
Paul Savage

The Citybus Leyland Lynxes spent much of their life in a dedicated livery for Northern Ireland Railways on the *Rail-Link* service to/from Belfast Central station. However, when this photograph was taken in October 1991, shortly before sale of the vehicle to Stevensons of Uttoxeter, No 3007 was on loan to Ulsterbus for use on the Derry Rail-Link service, for which it gained *NIR Inter City* rather than *NIR Suburban* fleet names.
Raymond Bell

The two Ulsterbus Leyland Lynxes were transferred to Citybus in 1989 and painted in standard livery. By the time this photo was taken in February 1991, No 3012 had also acquired the new fleetnames and logos, but it passed with the rest of the batch to Stevensons at the end of that year.
Paul Savage

The MCW Metroriders purchased for the *Airbus* service in 1988 were downgraded in 1991 and reappeared in *Busybus* livery, as illustrated by this photo of No 1804 beside the Guildhall in Londonderry that October. Most later served in the Flexibus fleet. Behind, Leyland Tiger No 1208, built specifically for Derry City services displays an overall advertising livery.
Raymond Bell

48

By 1989, apart from luxury coaches, a total of 270 Leyland Tigers with Alexanders 'N' type bodies had entered service, and there were orders for a further 90 in course of delivery, even before the major new order for Tiger chassis placed in 1988. Following the review of livery and corporate presentation, this type were to show more significant change of appearance, with more use of the ivory colour, especially along the roof and around the windscreen, to brighten the appearance of what had become a rather dowdy group of vehicles.

One of the last vehicles delivered in 1988 was No 1209, specified for Derry City services, and featuring experimental shaped plywood seats. This photograph, taken in October 1991, shows the original livery style applied to Leyland Tigers as well as the fleetname style which was unique to vehicles with this style of bodywork.
Raymond Bell

Another photograph of the same vehicle, taken in April 1995 also in Foyle Street, Derry, shows clearly the changes in livery and fleetname presentation, as well as the addition of 'Skybreaker' advertising panels. By this date also, the experimental seats had been replaced with standard bus seat frames.
Raymond Bell

This picture of Great Victoria Street-based Leyland Tiger No 1157 passing the war memorial in Lisburn in June 1994 typifies the effect of the livery changes upon the standard Alexander 'N' type bodywork, in this case without the addition of advertising. *Raymond Bell*

Thirty of the standard Leyland Tigers had received an upgraded specification of bodywork, with particular regard to the fitting of coach seating, for use primarily on Express services. One of these, No 465, is shown in original condition, leaving Glengall Street in August 1989. Construction of the multi-storey car park and Europa Buscentre is already well under way. *Paul Savage*

This photograph of Leyland Tiger express coach No 1130 shows the livery changes applied to that type, as well as the revised lettering style adopted for specially branded operations. This photograph was taken in May 1991 on the stands at Oxford Street bus station. Also visible are three standard Tigers and Leopard No 280, which, incidentally, is now preserved by Jeff Thompson of Newtownards. *Paul Savage*

Leyland Leopard No 215 is thought to have been the very last vehicle to have retained the old Ulsterbus livery. Having been allocated to Enniskillen, it was then moved to Dungiven, where it was snapped in January 1995 retaining the original shade of blue and the old transfers. *Author*

New vehicles 1989–2003

From 1989, Ulsterbus continued to receive Leyland Tigers with Alexanders N type bodywork, the balance of an outstanding order. Citybus, having failed to identify a suitable urban service bus to follow on from the Bristol RELL, also placed an order for the Leyland Tiger. However the specification for these differed from the Ulsterbus order in having Gardner engines and Taperlite springs rather than air suspension.

One of the Citybus Leyland Tigers, No 2605 is shown in Chichester Street in July 1988, shortly after entering service, in its original livery, the Citybus red version of the Ulsterbus livery applied to the N type bodywork.

Raymond Bell

By 1993, the same vehicle had acquired 'Skybreaker' advertising panels and the revised livery, complete with fleetname and logo. It was photographed in July 1993 in Donegall Square West.
John Goan

Many of this batch of buses have spent much of their lives decorated as overall advertisements. No 2627 is shown in August 1995, shortly after appearing with an overall design for Heinz Beans, which it was to carry for almost nine years.
John Goan

Some of the Citybus Tigers were later transferred to Ulsterbus, after delivery of low floor buses to Citybus commenced. No 2609 was captured by the camera in October 2001 in Great Victoria Street depot, preparing to perform a run to Poleglass on service 535, having been fully repainted into Ulsterbus colours.
Richard Whitford

53

Typical of the 1989 deliveries to Ulsterbus was Craigavon-allocated No 1250. This bus had been delivered in the older livery and was the last bus in Craigavon to be repainted into the later version. It was photographed as soon as this work had been completed, in July 1995.

John Goan

Many Ulsterbus vehicles of the 1989 delivery also appeared in advertising liveries. No 1282, allocated to Omagh, was promoting the Erneside shopping centre when it was photographed just outside the town's bus station in 1991.

John Goan

The next batch of Leyland Tigers for Ulsterbus, Nos 1300–1339, featured Volvo engines. Thirty-nine of these carried the Alexander N type body design, the exception being No 1321 (see page 58). One of the 39 N type-bodied buses, No 1317, allocated to Coleraine, was photographed in October 1993, near the Giant's Causeway.
Paul Savage

Another of the batch, No 1322, in a promotional livery for the Laganside Development Corporation is shown in May 1994 in the arrival bay at Oxford Street bus station, which had been rebuilt on a temporary basis to allow most of the site to be taken over for construction of the Waterfront Hall, one of the major development projects on Laganside.
John Goan

The last van conversions to roll out from the Ulsterbus workshops for their subsidiary company, Flexibus Limited, were four of the more powerful Mercedes 811D vehicles equipped with 19 luxury coach seats and larger luggage boots. Meanwhile the policy for small service buses for the *Busybus* fleet had changed from van conversions to slightly larger, purpose built vehicles with aluminium-framed coachbuilt bodies on Mercedes 709D chassis-cowls. Wrights were to secure a major order for 40 of their TS type bodies, delivered in 1989. These were followed by two further batches with the redesigned 'fast front' version of the TS body, delivered in 1991 and 1993.

Flexibus Mercedes 811D No 39 was one of the last four van conversions produced by Ulsterbus Engineering. These vehicles featured 19 luxury coach seats, curtains, forced air ventilation and an updated livery. No 39 is seen here on Laganbank Road, by the then Flexibus office, awaiting its next turn of duty. This area has changed beyond all recognition and is now part of the Lanyon Place development.

Paul Savage

The diffcrences between the original Wrights TS style of body and the later 'fast front' style are clearly shown in these views of the two types. Above is No 831, at Antrim Area Hospital, in April 1994, wearing an allover advert for Woodsides, a local store; below, outside the award winning Carrickfergus railway station, is 'fast front' No 881, from the third batch. *Paul Savage (above)/Norman Johnston (below)*

By 1990, Alexanders had completed a major redesign of the bodywork for Ulsterbus and Citybus vehicles, which was identified as the Q type, although Ulsterbus and Citybus initially adopted the 'Cityliner' name for these vehicles. Several types of seating were fitted to different batches, including reclining luxury coach seating fitted to one batch for use as Goldliner coaches. On completion of the Leyland Tiger chassis, the same body design was fitted to Volvo B10M chassis.

The 1990 prototype of the 'Q' type Alexanders body was fitted to No 1321, allocated to Antrim. It was photographed in O'Connell Street, Dublin in 1991 while operating a private hire journey. The livery of this vehicle was non-standard in that it did not display the blue fleet colour around the destination glass. Behind is a Dublin Bus Bombardier KD class double-decker. *Paul Savage*

This view of MkII Goldliner, No 1354 was taken at Letterkenny bus station, during the summer of 1992, when the vehicle was on loan to Bus Éireann and operating the Letterkenny–Dublin service. *Author*

58

This photograph of former MkII Goldliner No 1353, taken in Carnlough in 2001, reveals that, although relegated to service bus duty after 2000 and deprived of its gold stripe and Goldline lettering, it was still operating on the Goldline-branded *Antrim Coaster* service 252.   *Paul Savage*

This photograph of Cityliner No 2660 was taken on the first day of the new *City Express* service between Newtownabbey and Belfast in 1991. The vehicles carried the minimum of route branding at this stage.
                                                                                                                                                                                                Author

This photograph of No 2665 taken in Donegall Square West a little later, displays the route branding applied to the *City Express* route vehicles and publicity. *Raymond Bell*

Four of the Alexander Q type-bodied Tigers, Nos 2661–4, were allocated to the *Rail-Link* service to replace Leyland Lynxes. These Tigers had just 38 seats but large luggage pens over the front wheelarches. No 2663 is seen here in Belfast's Royal Avenue en route to Central Station. Officially service 100, this was rarely shown on vehicles, drivers instead displaying 'CL', which dated to when the service was branded *Citylink*. *Paul Savage*

No 2670, in standard livery, was photographed on Cregagh Road when first delivered to Citybus in 1991. All these vehicles originally displayed the 'Cityliner' model name on the front panel, although most were deleted within a year or two.
John Goan

After Stena Line moved their ferry terminal from Larne Harbour to Belfast with the introduction of the HSS *Stena Voyager* high speed ferry, Citybus were contracted to operate a connecting service between the city centre and the new terminal in Belfast docks. Two of the former *Rail-Link* Cityliners, Nos 2661 and 2662, were painted in a special promotional livery, although they were often to be found advertising Stena Line on normal Citybus services.
Raymond Bell

Few 'Cityliners' received advertising designs when they were new, but in later years this practice became quite prevalent This 1998 view of No 2663 illustrates one of the more complex designs, which also covers the side windows with a spotted film, through which passengers are able to see outwards – in theory, at least.
Raymond Bell

Fleet number No 2656 was one of the first batch of Cityliners delivered to Citybus in 1991. However it is shown here at Gilford, Co. Down shortly after being transferred to Ulsterbus in 1999, and before being repainted into Ulsterbus blue.
John Goan

62

This Leyland Tiger with Alexanders 'Q' type body, delivered to Ulsterbus in 1992 as No 1386, was still operating the trunk Belfast–Bangor route when it was photographed taking aboard some enthusiastic passengers at Cultra, some ten years later. *John Goan*

Delivery in 1992 of new 12m long coaches specifically for the very successful *City Express* route, also introduced the striking 'rainbow' livery and brand name style conceived for that service. These are well illustrated on No 1400 displayed at the Citybus-sponsored Balloon Carnival that year. *Raymond Bell*

After being displaced from the *City Express* route in 1996, No 1407 was given this special livery for Citybus Tours, also using the rainbow colours theme. Alongside, No 1401 is still displaying the small version of the *City Express* logo on its front panel.

Paul Savage

After the formation of Translink and the introduction of low floor Mercedes buses to the *City Express* route, the remaining 12m Tigers were demoted to ordinary bus service in Citybus and Ulsterbus. No 1406, is seen operating from Donegall Square West, in the simplified Citybus livery, devoid of lining.

Raymond Bell

No 1481 was one of the three 11m Leyland Tigers delivered to Citybus as additional vehicles for the *City Express* route with coach quality seating (though without the rainbow decals). Later in life it moved to Ulsterbus and received standard bus livery. It was photographed in 2001 in Belfast City centre. *Raymond Bell*

Typical of the standard Leyland Tigers with Alexanders 'Q' type bodywork delivered to Ulsterbus in 1992 is No 1453, depicted on a sunny afternoon in 1994 passing the King's Hall exhibition centre on the Lisburn Road.
Raymond Bell

Although delivered in 1992 as a standard service bus, No 1450 was photographed at Ballymena in the same year, operating the Northern Ireland portion of the longest Ulsterbus service, from Londonderry to London, a clear indication that the specification of these buses, when new, was considered good enough for coaching as well as bus work.
Paul Savage

A Cityliner of the 1992 delivery to Citybus, No 1465, was still displaying the 'Cityliner' transfer when photographed in 1995 operating on a special shuttle service from Stranmillis Embankment in conjunction with the Co-operation North Maracycle event. These vehicles were to the standard Ulsterbus specification, with air suspension and high back seating.
John Goan

This more recent photograph of a similar vehicle shows No 1470 operating a School Special journey on Gilnahirk Road.
Norman Johnston

Numerically the last of the Leyland Tigers to be delivered was No 1500, seen here at Bangor leaving the 1994 Irish Transport Trust Bus and Coach Rally.
Paul Savage

67

The Volvo B10M buses fitted with Alexander's 'Q' type bodies are not easily distinguished from the Leyland Tigers. This nearside view of the first of the Volvo batch, No 1501, shows the vented panel for the radiator on the nearside, a small clue.
Raymond Bell

This later view of No 1514, taken in Dungannon in 2000 shows the Translink decals and the simplification of the original livery which has befallen these fine buses in recent years. *John Goan*

During 1994, a batch of 40 Dennis Darts with Wrights Handybus bodies was delivered to Ulsterbus and Citybus. This model had proved very successful in England, even becoming established in Central London. In theory, the smaller dimensions and capacity were expected to prove very acceptable on some of the more remote rural routes, as well as some lightly loaded or tortuous routes in Belfast. In practice, it proved more difficult to find duties for which their capacity was adequate in peak hours. However, several were effectively used on services which had been established as *Busybus* routes but for which passenger demand had outstripped the capacity of the Mercedes midibuses.

Although retaining a few *Busybus* vehicles, many of the Bangor Town Services were operated by Dennis Darts, some replacing Leyland Leopards or Bristol RELLs. No 618 (together with Mercedes No 898) are shown in Bangor in 2000, during the period when the bus terminal was accommodated in Abbey Street car park, during the reconstruction of the Bangor rail and bus station facility.   *Norman Johnston*

No 601 was one of several Dennis Darts based at Lisburn which were given an adaptation of the *Busybus* livery, for use on the successful network of *Busybus* town services established there. The photograph was taken in Smithfield Square bus station in May 1994.
Raymond Bell

69

After some years, Dennis Darts in the Citybus fleet became associated with certain routes, including those on the Holywood Road, as indicated by No 634, photographed on a sunny day in November 2000.

Norman Johnston

Citybus No 624 was modified from new to accept wheelchairs and employed on a special group of services branded as *Easibus*, for elderly and disabled passengers. It was photographed near its base at Short Strand during July 1998.

Raymond Bell

A most unusual purchase in 1994 was a pair of articulated coaches. Van Hool Alizee bodywork graced the articulated bus version of the Volvo B10MA chassis. These provided greater capacity on the *City Express* service, but there is little doubt that the 'wow' factor was the main reason for their introduction. Both vehicles were eventually transferred to Ulsterbus and repainted into Goldliner livery.

Volvo B10MA artic No 3001 was an ideal medium on which to display the huge rainbow logo for the *City Express* service to full advantage. On this occasion, however, the vehicle was on loan to Ulsterbus, at Craigavon, for operation on service 250 between Portadown and Belfast via Sprucefield Shopping Centre.

Paul Savage

No 3001 was subsequently permanently transferred to Larne depot, and is seen here picking up passengers in Belfast's Bridge Street, bound for Larne on Goldline service 256.

Paul Savage

71

The first order for the new generation of ultra low floor buses comprised sixty Volvo B10L with Alexanders 'Ultra' bodies. This new model had been developed with close cooperation with Volvo and was to be constructed only at the Belfast factory. Two of the prototype vehicles were also purchased after periods of protracted loan to Citybus. Ten of the batch were allocated to Derry City Services, the remainder to Citybus in 1996.

No 2754, leaving the terminus of service D01 at Altnagelvin Hospital in March 1997, displays the version of the Ulsterbus livery adopted for low floor buses, in which these vehicles were supplied in 1996.

Raymond Bell

By the time this picture of No 2752 was taken in April 1999, the livery had acquired Translink decals.

Richard Whitford

However, the Derry based vehicles were soon being repainted into the Translink green livery introduced specifically for low floor buses. No 2753 was the subject of this picture taken in July 2001 as it emerges through the Ferryquay Gate in Derry's walls, illustrating very clearly why Derry City Services have been operated almost entirely with single-deck buses throughout their history. *Raymond Bell*

In Citybus, many of the 'Ultras' retained their original livery until well after the period covered by this volume. This photograph of No 2745, taken at the Dundonald (Ulster Hospital) terminus in January 2000 shows the original paint scheme, albeit with the addition of Translink decals, and a generous layer of winter roadgrit.
Norman Johnston

After delivery of the 'Ultras' there was some reluctance to commit to a repeat order. An order was placed with Mercedes for ten vehicles of their low floor O405 models – six rigids and four artics. Delivered in 1999, these had already been painted in the Citybus red and white livery, just before the Translink livery for low floor buses was decided upon, and they survived in that scheme for several years. These were intended for the *City Express*, though not offering the luxury coach quality of seating which passengers on this flagship service had enjoyed since 1992. However the articulated vehicles proved less suited to motorway service and were mainly used to offer increased seating capacity on the busy Antrim Road services.

Articulated Mercedes O405GN, No 3101 is shown at the outer end of the *City Express* route in August 2000, before these vehicles were displaced from the motorway service. *Norman Johnston*

No 2102, one of the rigid Mercedes O405Ns, displays the much reduced rainbow motif applied to these vehicles as collects its passengers at Donegall Square West in December 2000. *Paul Savage*

By August 2002 these vehicles were belatedly acquiring the Translink low floor livery. The *City Express* rainbow logo had been reduced in size yet again, and a 'Go' logo added as well. No 2100 is shown in Royal Avenue and although still 'dressed' for the *City Express* service it is arriving on the conventional service 48 from Newtownabbey, having been displaced from the premium service by new double-deckers. *Paul Savage*

Subsequent batches of low floor single-deck buses have comprised Volvo B10BLE chassis fitted with Wright Renown bodies, and Scania L94UB chassis with Wright Solar bodies. These types were supplied to both companies in the Translink standard livery for low floor buses, comprising two shades of green and small areas in the traditional company colour of red or blue.

No 2762 descends Gilnahirk Road en route from Mann's Corner to the City Centre in June 2000. This route was once covered by the Major Bus Company of WJ Clements, the only private bus operator in the Belfast area to survive compulsory acquisition on formation of the Northern Ireland Road Transport Board in 1935. Although the operation was acquired by Belfast Corporation in 1943, the Mann's Corner route extension beyond Gilnahirk was subsequently abandoned and was taken up, under political pressure, by the Ulster Transport Authority before being returned to Belfast Corporation in 1965, as part of a deal to allow buses which replaced trolleybuses on the Dundonald route to extend beyond the Elk Inn to terminate at the Ulster Hospital.

Norman Johnston

No 2774, one of four Volvo B10BLE low floor buses allocated to Ulsterbus specifically to operate new services between Carryduff and the City Centre as part of the Saintfield Road Quality Bus Corridor initiative introduced in 2000, is pictured in Botanic Avenue, Belfast sporting the 'Go' decals which distinguished the Quality Corridor services.

Raymond Bell

Citybus No 2793 was one of four vehicles operating the *Centrelink* service which were decorated with this route specific livery to promote the service, and Marks and Spencer, who contributed sponsorship to the service. It was photographed in August 2000 at the Central Station terminal of the service.
Norman Johnston

As the low floor buses rolled out to Ulsterbus depots around the province they started to appear on a wide variety of services. No 2827 was spotted in Scarva village en route from Portadown to Newry on service 63 in May 2001.
Raymond Bell

Outside Craigavon Hospital in May 2000, Craigavon depot driver Jim Magee negotiates No 2826 around one of the numerous roundabouts for which Craigavon is infamous.
John Goan

Ulsterbus No 738 was the last of the 2001 deliveries of Scania L94UB chassis with Wright Solar bodywork. It was actually one of three extra buses added to that year's order to cover for the closure of the Antrim–Lisburn branch rail line, but it is seen here at Upper Queen Street, Belfast after a journey from Lisburn on service 523.
Raymond Bell

In 1996 also, another batch of minibuses was purchased, with a view to the replacement of the original van conversions. This time Alexanders secured the order for their standard 'midibus' body, construction of which, at the time, was concentrated in their Belfast factory. The chassis cowl was the Mercedes 711D, an updated replacement for the previous 709D model.

One of the Alexander-bodied Mercedes, No 898, heads out from Bangor town centre towards Balloo Estate on the town service in August 1996. The single aperture destination display followed the precedent set by the early minibus conversions. Later however, Bangor vehicles received new destination screens which incorporated service numbers (see p69).
Paul Savage

A number of years were to pass before a manufacturer was to offer a 'midibus' which offered the accessibility advantages of the full size low floor bus. Optare achieved a neat and serviceable design with their 'Solo' model, of which a first batch was purchased in 2000.

Optare Solo No 1828 departs from Omagh bus station on the town service route to Lisanelly in June 2001.
Norman Johnston

79

The first new double-deckers to arrive on the streets of Belfast for more than twenty-five years were Volvo B7TL with Alexander ALX400 bodies. The first batch of 20 were delivered in 2001. Most, of course, were allocated to Citybus, but Ulsterbus received two for the very popular *University Link* (or *Unilink*) service.

Opposite top: Citybus No 2923 arrives at Four Winds terminus of service 84, bearing the 'Go' logos which were introduced to distinguish the 'Quality Corridor' services introduced on the Saintfield Road.

Norman Johnston

Opposite bottom: The *City Express* service was also taken over largely by the new double-deckers and classed as a Quality Corridor. No 2940 is shown in Royal Avenue in August 2002, bearing both the 'Go' and the *City Express* logos.

Paul Savage

Loadings on the *University Link* service had increased to such an extent that double-deck operation became the only sensible way forward and, consequently, Volvo B7TLs Nos 2931 and 2932 were transferred from Citybus to Ulsterbus. On Saturday 2 December 2001, No 2932 was, however, used to provide additional capacity on the Belfast to Lisburn service. It is seen here passing Lambeg, on what is believed to have been the first double-deck working between the two cities for over ten years!

Paul Savage

It was intended that all 20 of this batch of Volvo B7TL double-deckers would be delivered to Citybus and, indeed, all arrived with red stripes and swoops. However, two, Nos 2935 and 2936, never actually saw service with Citybus, being repainted blue and transferred to Ulsterbus, so the photograph of No 2936 in the red scheme (below) is particularly rare. Ballygomartin must have been the longest single destination name that would be displayed on these vehicles but, if you look closely, the side display is showing Ballygowan!

Paul Savage

The two Ulsterbus Volvo B7TLs, Nos 2935 and 2936, are posed together in October 2001 in Great Victoria Street depot, shortly after delivery, displaying the service destinations for the *Unilink* service.

Richard Whitford

82

Yes, believe it! This unusual vehicle is part of the Ulsterbus fleet! The Gentrac Road Train, allocated No 2900, was purchased in 1996 for use around Portrush, and was photographed there in August 2000.
Raymond Bell

This double-deck luxury coach, an unusual purchase by Citybus in 1999 for the Belfast City Tour, is an Ayats Bravo 1. Later, Translink abandoned the City Tours programme, and the vehicle became a Goldline coach, based at Londonderry, where it has given excellent service. In this photograph, taken in August 2000 at the Castle Junction City Tour departure point, No 2001 is accompanied by Alexander-bodied Daimler Fleetline No 2863, which was delivered in 1973, maliciously destroyed in the same year, and rebodied in 1974. It was converted to open-top layout in 1991.
Raymond Bell

An unusual acquisition by Ulsterbus was the former NIRTB and UTA Leyland Tiger PS1, A515, dating from 1947. Already a towing vehicle when absorbed into the Ulsterbus fleet in 1967, it was sold for preservation in 1977. After restoration as a bus, it had been with several owners before being acquired by Ulsterbus in 1997, and placed in the care of its original restoring owner, Robert McMaster of Antrim depot, who is visible in this photograph taken at the Bus and Coach rally at Antrim in 1998. *Author*

Typical of the community minibuses which Translink maintains on behalf of the Department for Regional Development, are Mercedes 410D CCZ 6068 and Renault Master CCZ 6074, photographed at Craigavon depot in March 2002. Both have panel van bodywork converted by Nu-Track of Antrim.

Norman Johnston

A small number of Dennis Dart SLF midibuses, with Wright Crusader bodies, were purchased in 1997 for extension of the *Easibus* service concept, both in Citybus and in Ulsterbus territory. No 644, one of those intended for the (blue) Ulsterbus fleet is shown fully lettered for *Easibus*, but carrying trade plates, before entering service.
Author

Three more Dennis Dart SLF, with Wright Crusader bodies, were delivered in 1999. Even shorter than the previous vehicles, these were intended as replacements for some Mercedes 709D midibuses which had been maliciously destroyed, but were instead allocated to new city centre operations in Belfast. No 646, operated by Citybus, provided a shuttle service for patients and visitors between the city centre and the Royal Hospitals. The photograph, taken in January 2000, shows the special contract livery, adapted from the original Ulsterbus/Citybus low floor livery, in which these buses were delivered, but with Translink logos.
Raymond Bell

The other two, Nos 645/7 were delivered in Ulsterbus low floor livery, which was adapted to incorporate service specific lettering and logos for the Northside (No 645) and Eastside (No 647) Park and Ride services, operated by Flexibus, on behalf of DRD Roads Service. This view of No 645 was taken in Royal Avenue, at the city centre end of the route. It is interesting to note that Nos 645 and 647 are the only vehicles in the combined fleets to proclaim their low floor credentials. *Paul Savage*

Opposite top: The *Airlink* service to Belfast City Airport was upgraded in 2002 with the introduction of coach-seated Optare Solos in a dedicated livery. No 1837 is seen passing Belfast's City Hall, with the Scottish Provident building in the background, on a working to the airport in June 2003. *Paul Savage*

Opposite bottom: The Flexibus coaching fleet received four of these Plaxton Cheetah-bodied Mercedes, Nos 1–4, in 2002. These luxurious vehicles seat just 24 passengers. No 4 is seen in Belfast's Royal Avenue in August 2002 when on a fairly mundane duty; it was being used as a crew transfer vehicle for the drivers on the park and ride shuttles! *Paul Savage*

The next orders for small buses comprised a substantial batch of Optare Solos and a quartet of Plaxton Cheetah coaches.

Newtownards-based Optare Solo No 1860 is seen at Oxford Street, Belfast in June 2003, on a service 5C working from Laganside Buscentre to Newtownards via Craigantlet. This batch of Solos was delivered in the 'swoopless' version of the Translink livery, where the blue flash, which swept over the rear wheels, was omitted.
Paul Savage

Solo No 1870 was also allocated to Newtownards. It is seen here at the town's shopping centre working a local service to Beverley Heights, on the north side of the town. On this occasion the bus was unable to use the dedicated turning circle due to inconsiderately-parked cars.
Paul Savage

Pre-owned vehicles acquired 1989–2003

Eleven Leyland Leopard/Alexander Y-type buses were purchased from companies in the Scottish Bus Group in 1988/9. These were intended primarily for driver tuition, as they were fitted with manual gearboxes. This was also the preferred specification for buses converted by the engineering department into towing vehicles, a use to which several of the Scottish buses passed after training needs were reduced.

Only one of the Leyland Leopards acquired from the Scottish Bus Group, No 1885, OSJ 613R was used in passenger service, operating a schools contract at Armagh depot during 1996/7. No 1885 had been new to Western Scottish in late 1976 but was acquired from Clydeside Scottish in 1989. *Raymond Bell*

More typical of the use made of the Scottish Leopards was this ex Central Scottish bus, No 1881 (MHS 20P) in driving school livery. The three vehicles in this batch carried the short window bay version of the Alexander Y-type body.
Raymond Bell

When they first arrived the Scottish Leopards displayed a variety of versions of the Ulsterbus livery, some derived from the most economic means of covering their original colours. Fleet number 1889 (RAG 389M), in this photograph taken in 1989, displays almost exactly the livery applied by Ulsterbus to its first Y-type coaches, the Potter-built Wolfhounds, in 1967.
Richard Whitford

This Leyland Leopard No 1886 (OSJ 620R) originally served with Western SMT and later with Clydeside Scottish. While performing its driving training duties, it was 'dressed up' as a Midland Scottish example, based upon its Ulsterbus livery, to feature in a film. It was photographed at Belfast's City Hall in December 1994, before regaining Ulsterbus fleetnames. It was subsequently purchased for preservation.
Raymond Bell

No 1887 (RAG 383M), ex Northern Scottish (although originally Western SMT), was initially allocated for training duties and reliveried simply by painting blue over the previous owner's yellow. This livery was very reminiscent of the original 1967 Ulsterbus scheme applied to former UTA buses. The photograph was taken in April 1989 at the annual Bus Rally at Carrickfergus, very shortly after introduction of the vehicle into training school service.

Richard Whitford

Several years later, in 1992, and the same vehicle, after being neatly shortened, was allocated to Downpatrick depot as the engineering vehicle. By this time also it had acquired the Leyland Tiger version of the latest livery.

Author

A batch of twelve Leyland Atlantean AN68/1R double-deckers with Eastern Coach Works bodywork which had originated with Sheffield and District, was purchased from a dealer in the south of England in 1989. All were reregistered on arrival, eleven receiving marks originally booked for the Mark I Goldliners, which had been delayed. Initially used as conventional double-deckers, mainly on heavy school transport services, many saw further service in other guises.

No 907 (OXI 517) is pictured at Ballygawley, Co Tyrone, on completion of its afternoon journey from Omagh in May 1992. These vehicles were later re-numbered in the 2900-series to make way for the batch of Alexander-bodied Mercedes 711D minibuses. *John Goan*

After conversion to open-top configuration, and dressed overall in an advertising livery, No 2906 (OXI 516) prepares to leave Bangor on the open-top service to Ballywalter in 1995. *Raymond Bell*

No 2904 (OXI 514) was equipped in 1993 not only as an open topper, but also to carry wheelchairs, for the Silent Valley shuttle service, where it was photographed on a very busy day in March 1997.

John Goan

No 2912 (OXI 529) was converted into a 'wedding coach', and was photographed shortly after completion of the alterations in March 1993.

Raymond Bell

93

No 2901 became a glass-roofed tour bus with Citybus in 1991, and was photographed outside the former Park Parade School (since demolished) in March 1999.
Raymond Bell

No 2901 was later converted to part open-top, after several of the specially-shaped glass panes were broken. The bus is seen here in June 2003 in Donegall Square East, passing the Titanic Memorial in the City Hall grounds. *Paul Savage*

No 2911 was converted to open-top in 1997, and was undertaking duties as a tree-lopping vehicle when caught by the photographer on Stranmillis Road in October 2002.
Raymond Bell

The purchase of second-hand ECW-bodied Bristol REs which had been such a notable feature of the 1980s for the Citybus fleet, had virtually ceased by 1988. A few of those purchased in 1988 entered service in 1989, and one further batch was acquired in that year. However destruction of the Citybus fleet had reduced and few of these were used in service. The last remaining vehicles of this type were taken out of service by 1990. A few of these, together with some unused vehicles from the reserve stock were resold for further use, or preservation, in England.

No 764 (NCK 338J) was pressed into service late in 1988 in its original owner's livery (Ribble Motor Services). Photographed here in Donegall Place in February 1989, it was later painted into full Citybus livery and remained in service until 1990. It is now preserved in Great Britain. *Paul Savage*

Although purchased in 1987 from Crosville Wales, No 748 (EFM 181H) did not enter service until August 1989, when it was photographed in Upper Queen Street. It was subsequently acquired for preservation by a group based in Cheshire.

Paul Savage

This vehicle, No 769 (LTG 35L) was a Bristol RESL, with Leyland engine, acquired from Yelloway in 1988 and featured the rare single line destination display. It is seen here in Donegall Square West. The vehicle entered service in August 1989, but was withdrawn at the end of the same month.
Paul Savage

Fleet No 778 (WNG 864H) was acquired in 1988 from Cambus. Although a rather early model, as indicated by the flat windscreens, it was painted into full Citybus livery, but in the event was used only on driver training duties. It is seen in November 1989 in Chichester Street on a section of road which, shortly after, was closed to all traffic for security reasons, and to this day remains closed, necessitating a lengthy and time-consuming diversion for many Citybus services.
Paul Savage

In 1989, Northern Ireland Railways purchased five Leyland Tiger/Van Hool Alizee luxury coaches previously operated by Shearings. From the outset, responsibility for the maintenance and operation of these coaches was contracted to Ulsterbus, where they were based at Craigavon and Newry depots, to be available for all too frequent substitution of the 'Enterprise' trains between Belfast and Dublin. The initial livery applied the then current NIR 'Inter City' colours over the livery layout used by their former owner. Ownership passed to Ulsterbus in 1991 and Ulsterbus fleetnames soon appeared, later followed by complete repainting of the vehicles into the Ulsterbus coaching livery.

No 595 (OXI 525) awaits passengers at Central Station during its first few days of operation, late in 1989.
Author

A year later, in 1990, No 592 (OXI 522) heads a group of railway replacement vehicles awaiting passengers outside Lurgan station.
John Goan

Nos 591–3 (OXI 521–3) are shown in their original colours but with Ulsterbus names on the front panels, at Craigavon depot in 1992.

Raymond Bell

By the time No 591 (OXI 521) was photographed in Dunfanaghy, Co Donegal, in 1995, it had been repainted into the standard Ulsterbus coach livery of the period, and was lettered for Ulsterbus Coach Hire.

Paul Savage

During the winter of 1989/90, Ulsterbus also required to increase its luxury coach fleet, and went to dealers for second-hand stock. From the Shearings fleet came three Van Hool-bodied Leyland Tigers similar to those purchased by NIR, together with four Plaxton-bodied Tigers. However, there were not sufficient Leyland Tiger coaches available and the company also acquired six DAF MB200/MB230 coaches with a selection of Duple and Plaxton body styles.

No 500 (RXI 5500), was one of the Plaxton-bodied Leyland Tigers, and had originally been No 499 (B499 UNB) in the fleet of Smiths Shearings of Wigan.
Paul Savage

From the same source, No 598 (RXI 5598) a Leyland Tiger with Van Hool 'Alizee' coachwork is seen arriving in Blackpool with a private party from Northern Ireland in August 1995. *Raymond Bell*

99

This DAF MB230 with Duple 340 coach body, acquired through the Hughes DAF dealership, had previously seen service with Hanmer of Wrexham, before becoming No 686 (RXI 6686) in the Ulsterbus Tours fleet. It was based for many years at the Stranraer depot and on this occasion, in October 1994, was parked up in Glasgow.
Raymond Bell

No 681 (RXI 6681) is a DAF MB200DKFL with Duple Caribbean II bodywork, one of three similar coaches previously operated by London Coaches. It was one of two painted in Scottish Citylink livery with the 'The Ulsterman' name, to operate on the Stranraer–London express coach service. It is seen in Buckingham Palace Road, approaching the London terminal of the service. *Raymond Bell*

100

A second shot of No 681 (RXI 6681), this time inside Victoria Coach Station, as it awaits departure time for the 425-mile journey to Stranraer.
Paul Savage

The same vehicle was subsequently repainted in a simplified version of the coaching livery. At this stage, although normally used on driver training duties, the vehicle was a regular performer on Friday afternoons on the cross-border service from Belfast to Cavan/Galway. It is pictured at Galway in August 1994 resting in the Bus Éireann depot, beside Bus Éireann Bombardier KE 27 (27 VZJ), originally a tour coach for CIÉ Tours International and subsequently used on *Expressway* services.
Raymond Bell

This West Midlands Travel Iveco, with Carlyle body, was one of four leased during 1992. Although the owner's livery of white with a dark blue skirt was retained, some were lettered for Flexibus, others for *Busybus* operation. No 48 (E513 TOV), lettered for Flexibus, was photographed in October 1992.
Raymond Bell

Around this time, the opportunity was taken to acquire a Mercedes with Alexander bodywork, which had previously been a manufacturer's demonstration vehicle and which had already spent some time with Flexibus. Allocated No 42 (MXI 6786), it was photographed in Europa Buscentre during the summer of 1993, when it was carrying special branding for the 'Lagan Pony', an experimental park and ride service which operated that year. *Raymond Bell*

In 1990, Ulsterbus acquired the Strabane town service which had been introduced by M Donnell of Strabane, together with two of his Mercedes vehicles.

LJI 4646 is shown here in Donnell's livery a few months before acquisition. As this vehicle was a coach, unsuited to operation on the town service, it was allocated to the Flexibus fleet, as No 43. It was burnt out in a malicious incident in 1995.
Ian Houston

MJI 3341, with Alexander (Falkirk) body, became No 44. It was quickly repainted into the *Busybus* livery and had its seating capacity reduced from 33 to 25. It was photographed in August 1990 whilst in Portrush on a private hire. It was soon transferred away from the Strabane and Londonderry area, although it remained in the Ulsterbus fleet for more than ten years, mainly in Newtownards.
Paul Savage

In 1991 it was decided that Citybus should have a modern double-deck luxury coach for the Belfast City Tour. After a search around the second-hand market, a DAF SBR2300DHS with Van Hool Astrobel body was acquired from Berryhurst International Travel of London, a company specialising in transport of pop groups and bands, for which the vehicle had originally been convertible to carry sleeping berths on the upper deck. In the same year the group took its first steps to experiment with articulated vehicles. A Leyland-DAB of South Yorkshire Transport was leased for several months, primarily to provide high capacity transport for the Tall Ships event in Belfast in June of that year.

DAF SBR2300/Van Hool No 2000 (UXI 2000) is on display in Bangor Castle grounds during the Irish Transport Trust Bus and Coach Rally in April 1991, shortly after acquisition. *John Goan*

A second and more colourful livery had been adopted for Citybus Tours and applied to No 2000 by the time this photograph was taken at the 1994 Bus and Coach Rally at Carrickfergus.
Raymond Bell

104

Right: The Leyland DAB articulated bus performs its crowd-shifting task outside the dock gates in Garmoyle Street, Belfast in June 1991. It was given the fleet number 2001 for the duration of its stay.
Author

Below: This picture reveals in greater detail the promotional livery applied to No 2001 to give advance publicity to the Tall Ships event.
Raymond Bell

105

Between 1992 and 1995, Ulsterbus had a pressing need to develop its midibus fleet, partly to handle increased contracts and services around the provincial depots and partly to improve the fleet available to its Flexibus subsidiary in Belfast, which had received its last new vehicles some three years before. A varied collection of used Mercedes buses and coaches were purchased. Most of these were re-registered soon after acquisition. Full details are included in the fleet lists.

Fleet No 49 (XXI 1670) was a Mercedes 811D with fairly rare PMT body, acquired through Chambers, Moneymore. It is here photographed at the ITT Rally in Bangor in 1993. *John Goan*

And here's the same vehicle in July 2001 displaying the more recent Flexibus livery of white with deep purple-blue and Translink turquoise.
Ian Houston

No 51 was acquired from Ian Houston of Newtownards when he ceased operation. It is shown outside Duncrue Street workshops ready to enter service with Flexibus. It was one of two of the acquired Mercedes to sport Made to Measure body conversions. After withdrawal it was re-purchased by its original owner, for preservation.
Ian Houston

Fleet No 52 (FAZ 3052) was another Mercedes which had previously been a manufacturer's demonstrator. This small vehicle, with Devon body conversion was ideal for a school transport contract secured by Coleraine depot. The photograph taken in 2001 shows the final version of its livery with Translink decals.
Author

Fleet no 63 (GAZ 2063) was one of four Mercedes 609D with Reeves Burgess body conversions acquired through Chambers of Moneymore. These had originally been courtesy buses operated by Hertz at London Airport. The wide doorway made them particularly suitable for some types of service, and this vehicle bore a special livery for a service to Belfast City Airport in 1995.
Raymond Bell

Two Mercedes 811D with Whittaker bus bodies were purchased through a dealer in Victoria Bridge, Co Tyrone, who had acquired a fleet of coaches previously used to operate staff transport for the Weetabix factories in eastern England. No 56 (H643 UWE) was photographed in August 1994, when ready to enter service on a school contract service, still in the Weetabix yellow livery. *Raymond Bell*

This picture of No 56, carrying *Busybus* lettering, was taken at Newry station in March 2000 when operating the 'Linkline' connection between the station and the town centre.
John Goan

Flexibus No 60 (FAZ 3060) was one of two coaches with Plaxton Beaver bodywork purchased from Chambers of Moneymore. It is seen in an experimental livery applied in 1999, but not adopted.

Raymond Bell

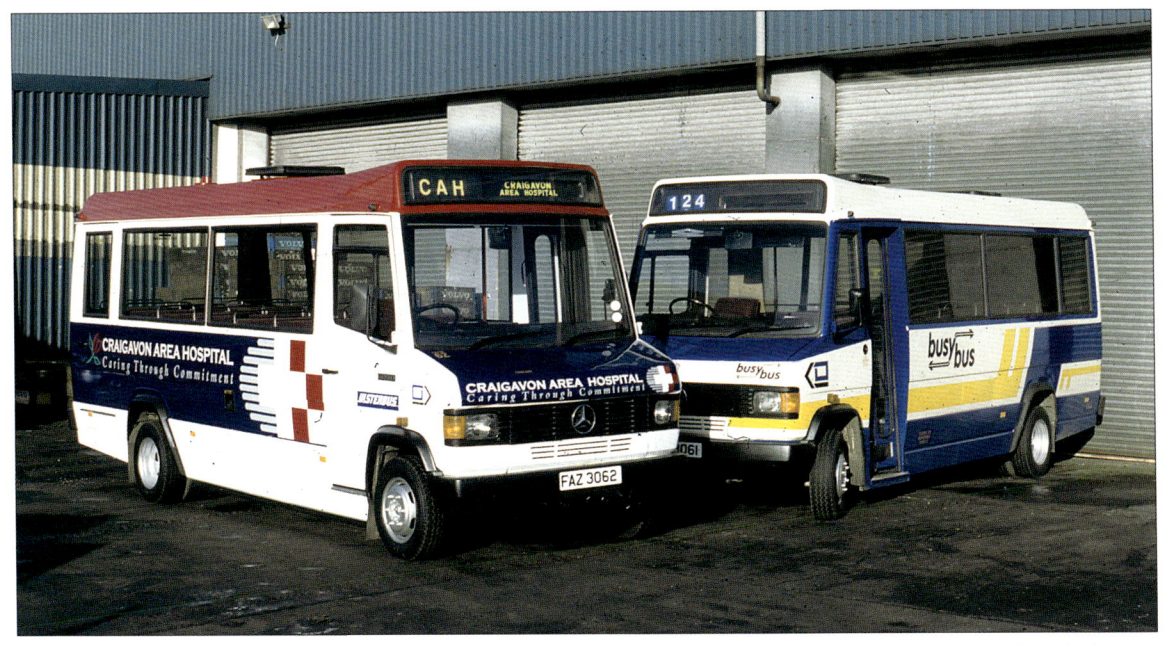

Two standard Mercedes midibuses with Reeve Burgess body conversion were purchased, through a dealer, from North Western Road Car. No 62 (FAZ 3062) was given a dedicated livery for a new contract service between Banbridge and Craigavon Hospital, operated on behalf of the Craigavon Hospital Trust, while No 61 (FAZ 3061) was given standard *Busybus* livery. Both are shown outside Duncrue Street workshops in 1994.

Raymond Bell

During 1992, Ulsterbus acquired the fleet of buses operated by Martyrs Memorial Church, Belfast, and provided the services on a contract hire basis. It had not been intended to operate any of the buses, but at the time there was a shortage of buses with manual gearboxes for driver training, and four of the acquired fleet, all Bristol LHs, were earmarked for possible reinstatement as training vehicles. In the event only two were so treated. A similar exercise was carried out in 1994 when the fleet operated by Metropolitan Tabernacle, Whitewell, Belfast was replaced by contract hire operation, but on this occasion none of the vehicles were either suitable, or required, for further use.

This photograph shows both vehicles, No 1892 (SWS 774S) and No 1893 (GPD 301N) as they were turned out for driving instruction. The second (nearest the camera) was a shorter vehicle on a Bristol LHS chassis and had been given a neatly made non-standard replacement windscreen by a previous owner. As it transpired, both vehicles were also used in passenger service for limited periods and both were subsequently acquired for preservation.

Raymond Bell

Opposite top: During its demonstration period with Citybus, Neoplan No 2009 (K930 EWG) operated in Merseyside 'Smartbus' livery. The photograph is taken in York Street in March 1994. Although the front destination display shows Citybus service 64 to Downview, it appears that removal of the Merseyside destination from the side display has been overlooked!

Raymond Bell

Opposite bottom: After acquisition, this vehicle unusually retained its fleet number in the demonstrator series; it was also later re-registered with a matching Northern Ireland mark, IAZ 2009. The initial livery, with its cartoon legs, was intended to emphasise the low floor design. It is shown operating on Ulsterbus service 41 between Bessbrook and Newry in August 1995.

Raymond Bell

By 1993/4 the bus manufacturing industry was working hard on improving accessibility to buses. The future was seen to lie in ultra low floor designs, with only a single step up from ground level. Among the vehicles obtained as demonstrators was a German-built Neoplan which had already been supplied as a prototype for the Smartbus project in Merseyside. This vehicle was purchased to give longer term operating experience. After its demonstration visit in Citybus it was painted into Ulsterbus livery and used in Newry and Bangor, before eventually being converted into a safety promotion and training vehicle in Translink low floor livery.

Much later the bus was repainted into a simplified version of the Translink low floor bus livery and was photographed in Bangor in April 2000. *Raymond Bell*

The final chapter for this vehicle was conversion into a safety promotion and training unit, in which guise it was photographed in Lady Dixon Park, Belfast in November 2001. *Raymond Bell*

Meanwhile the British bus industry was also developing low floor designs. Alexanders went into partnership with Volvo to produce a version of the B10L low floor bus, already in production in Sweden, and the local Belfast factory was chosen to assemble the model, called the Ultra. Several prototypes were built, of which one quickly entered service with Citybus, initially as a demonstrator, although later purchased. Another of the prototypes, which had been used for testing and development, but had not been registered for road use, was later supplied to Citybus on a similar basis, and eventually purchased. Both vehicles initially projected a promotional image, combining the Citybus low floor livery with Alexanders' promotional lettering.

The first protype, No 2700 (HAZ 4809), is seen at the Ladybrook terminus in August 1996. Unlike the production vehicles, both prototypes had one piece windscreens, and more prominent cooling vents at the offside rear. *Raymond Bell*

The second prototype to enter service became No 2761 in the Citybus fleet, with matching MAZ 3761 registration. In this 1996 photograph, it is shown negotiating the awkward turn from Cherryvalley into Cherryvalley Park, on the long-standing route to Gilnahirk and Mann's Corner originally provided by the Major Bus Service. Due to the increasing size of modern buses, the route has since been altered to omit this section.
Raymond Bell

As driver training continued to require vehicles with manual gearboxes, Ulsterbus kept an eye open for suitable vehicles on the second-hand market.

This ex Royal Navy Leyland Tiger, with Wadham Stringer body, turned up in the sales stock of commercial vehicle dealer Patterson's of Ballygawley in 1995 and proved very suitable for training purposes. However, it was given a full PSV licence and appeared, from time to time, on passenger-carrying service. On this occasion, No 540 (HAZ 3540) was waiting in Corporation Square for a private hire party from the Seacat cross-channel ferry. *Paul Savage*

Another vehicle purchased for training purposes was this Leyland-DAB articulated bus, one of a fleet previously operated by British Airways for airside transport. No 2999 (RLN 231W) was fully repainted in a version of the training livery in 1996, but saw little use, as the licensing authority decided that existing PCV drivers would not need to be re-tested to drive articulated buses. *Raymond Bell*

Touring Coaches

The Tours Department operates a fleet of very high quality Luxury Touring Coaches from its Glengall Street, Belfast base, and its sub-depot at Stranraer in Scotland. A range of popular Extended Tours now covers much of Continental Europe as well as Ireland and Britain. Cross-channel express services between Belfast, Stranraer and major British cities are also operated, mainly by Stranraer.

The purchase of small numbers of specially equipped luxury touring coaches for the long distance touring activities operated most successfully by the Belfast based 'Tours Department' continued throughout the period under review. Sometimes these were included in bulk vehicle purchases and sometimes taken as separate orders, in those circumstances often showing a willingness to take models which had not previously featured in the company's standardised purchasing policy.

No 679 was one the first batch of DAF MB230 / Plaxton Paramount 3500 coaches to be purchased by Ulsterbus Tours in 1990. Although photographed in Carrickfergus, soon after delivery, it was based in Stranraer, and is being driven on this occasion by John Finningham, lead driver at that location.

Richard Whitford

No 680, of the same batch was photographed in August 2000 in Edinburgh, preparing to leave from the temporary stand at St Andrew's Square, on the cross-channel express service to Belfast via Stranraer. By this time it had been repainted in the later Tours livery, incorporating a green stripe as well as two shades of blue.
Raymond Bell

In the twilight of her Ulsterbus career DAF MB230 coach No 672, was transferred to Great Victoria Street for use as an express services coach. It was photographed passing along Belfast's Royal Avenue in May 2003 when on an *Airbus* duty from Belfast International Airport at Aldergrove.
Paul Savage

No 671 was one of the third batch of DAF coaches, delivered in 1993. Allocated to Stranraer, it was operating on the cross-channel express service to/from Middlesbrough (service 928), when photographed in Newcastle upon Tyne in 1996. *Raymond Bell*

Ulsterbus returned to Volvo for its luxury coach purchases in 1994, with two B10M chassis fitted with Plaxton Excalibur bodies. With these vehicles came a new livery, incorporating an additional green stripe and a flamboyant wave. No 505 (below) was photographed in May 1994 at Stranmillis during the Belfast Lord Mayor's Show. *Paul Savage*

117

A further five similar vehicles were added during the following year. No 509, of this batch, was photographed in Howard Street, Belfast in June 2001.
Paul Savage

No 512, one of the pair of short Volvo B10M with Caetano Algarve II bodies delivered in 1996, was caught by the photographer outside the garage at Stranraer on 16 July 2003.
Raymond Bell

The gap between the Volvo coaches and the Goldliners in the fleet numbering system having been closed, the next group of Volvo coaches to arrive were given numbers adjoining the DAF coaches. No 692 represents the 1999 deliveries of B10M/Plaxton Excalibur coaches, photographed when new at Cultra.
Richard Whitford

118

Having built up a substantial fleet of Plaxton Excalibur coaches, it was, perhaps, inevitable that the Tours Department would look elsewhere for a more distinctive design for the new millennium, after the Excalibur had been chosen for Goldline service coaches. Thus, the 2001 coaches, still on Volvo B10M chassis, had Caetano Enigma bodywork. The five vehicles in this order, Nos 695–9 (ICZ 6695–9) were delivered in plain white, the stripes and fleetnames being applied at Falls Park depot in Belfast where No 699 is seen in May 2001.
Paul Savage

No 699, now adorned with full Ulsterbus Tours livery, is seen here at Foyle Street, Derry, in the company of another Volvo product B10L No 2755 with Alexander Ultra bodywork.
Paul Savage

119

Another major change in purchasing policy occurred prior to the 2002 deliveries, when orders were switched to Scania for the K114 chassis, and for the body order, to Irizar, for their Century model. No 101 was photographed at the Lagan Lookout, Belfast, during an Irish Transport Trust outing in October 2002. Colourpoint authors Billy Montgomery and Michael Collins are waiting to board. *Norman Johnston*

No less than eight more coaches of the Scania/Irizar Century type were added to the fleet in 2003. Of these, No 109 was one of two delivered in Eurolines livery for operation on the cross-channel express services. It is shown leaving Stranraer Harbour with its passenger load from the Stena HSS fast ferry.
Raymond Bell

No 110 was delivered in plain white, with just the addition of Ulsterbus Tours fleetnames, in blue, for use as the spare coach on both the Eurolines and Scottish Citylink duties. It is seen outside the garage at Stranraer in July 2003.
Raymond Bell

No 111, another of the same batch, displays the Scottish Citylink livery applied for operation on the Belfast–Stranraer–Glasgow cross-channel express service. This coach also works a Glasgow to Dunblane service for Scottish Citylink in the evening, returning to Glasgow early the following morning. *Trevor Dixon*

Goldline

The last twenty Leyland engined Tiger chassis were supplied to Ulsterbus in 1989/90. Sixteen of these received Alexander 'TE' type bodywork with reclining luxury coach seats, to form the first batch of Express service coaches which were used, under the new 'Goldline' branding, to revolutionise the operation of the company's many fast limited stop services across the province.

Prior to their entry into service all 16 of the Goldliners were taken to Foyle Street bus station, Londonderry for a 'photo opportunity' with the city's famous Guildhall as a backdrop. *Ulsterbus*

Opposite top: Five of the new Goldliner coaches are parked together in Great Victoria Street depot yard, in May 1990, shortly after entering service. Nearest the camera is No 515. *Paul Savage*

Opposite bottom: Fleet number 1351, one of the Mark II vehicles, is resplendent in delivery condition as it takes part in the annual Bus and Coach Rally at Carrickfergus in 1991 shortly after delivery.

Richard Whitford

Relaunching of the Express service network as 'Goldline' was so successful that there was an urgent need to increase the strength of the Goldline fleet beyond the initial batch of sixteen. The quickest way to achieve this, with the willing co-operation of the Alexander factory in Belfast, was to step up the specification of a batch of the Leyland Tigers with Alexander 'Q' type bodies which were already ordered. Accordingly, twenty were fitted out as Mark II Goldliners, with reclining coach seats and the now familiar Goldline livery. Due to the 11 metre length of these vehicles, the seating capacity was limited to 49, but this was quite adequate for many of the express services at the time.

123

While the Mark II vehicles provided some respite, a further batch of full size (12 metre) Goldliner Express coaches was required, and the contract this time was awarded to Robert Wright and Sons, who produced a new body, named 'Endeavour', mounted on Volvo-engined Leyland Tiger chassis, to become the Mark III Goldliners, delivered in 1992.

This view of No 1420, a Mark III Goldliner, was taken at the Mall, Armagh. in April 1997, having performed a journey from Belfast on the 'Orchard Express' service 251, despite the fact that the vehicle is lettered for the 'Lakeland Express' service 261 operated by Enniskillen depot. It will, however, work through to Enniskillen on service 193, serving Caledon, Aughnacloy and Ballygawley en route. The higher roofline of the Wright Endeavour body compared with the standard Alexander-bodied service bus behind is clearly visible.

John Goan

The company now had sufficient confidence in the 'Goldline' brand to realise that the purchase of traditional luxury coach bodywork instead of the high specification dual purpose vehicles used so far, would be most appropriate. By this time, the Leyland Tiger chassis had been discontinued by its Volvo owners and future purchases were of the Volvo B10M model. Plaxton secured the next two contracts, the Premier coach body being supplied on 50 vehicles in 1994 and a further 30 in 1996. These were known as the Mark IV Goldliners.

This early photograph of the first of the Plaxton-bodied Goldliners, No 1551, in showroom condition, was taken for publicity purposes before it entered service.
Ulsterbus

Two of the Mark IV Goldliners were transferred to Citybus as tours and private hire coaches. No 1572 waits for its load at Castle Place before starting on a Belfast City Tour, in June 2002.
Raymond Bell

The second group of Mark IV Goldliners is represented by No 1605, photographed at Ballymena in February 2001, en route to Portrush. *Richard Whitford*

In 1996, the company introduced two articulated Goldliners to provide additional capacity, and visual appeal on the busiest Goldline services. Van Hool Alizee coachwork was mounted on the articulated coach version of the Volvo B10MA chassis. These were later joined by the two articulated coaches purchased in 1994 for Citybus, and although fitted with fixed rather than reclining seats, these were painted up in full Goldline livery.

The articulated coaches were usually to be found on the services from Newry and Londonderry to Belfast. No 3002 is seen at Foyle Street Buscentre, Londonderry, in July 2002. *Richard Whitford*

Opposite: This group of Goldliners parked on layover at Europa Buscentre in May 1994 illustrate the differences between the first four Marks. From the left are Mark IV No 1562, Mark III No 1413, Mark II No 1351 and Mark I No 516. *Raymond Bell*

The next major order was for top of the range Plaxton Excalibur coaches, delivered in 1999. Twenty, 53 seaters, became the Mark V Goldliners, and another ten, with 49/51 seats and toilet compartments, were the Mark VI Goldliners. These were intended primarily for the cross-border and cross-channel express services together with private hire and tours. This contract introduced a new version of the Goldline livery, although no attempt has been made to apply this livery to earlier vehicles.

Opposite top: No 1653, one of the Mark V Goldliners stands in the parcels bay at Belfast's Europa Buscentre after a journey from Derry via Omagh to Belfast on service 273 in September 1999. The revised Goldline livery is very dignified although the gold wave, in contrast with the blue, is less prominent. *Raymond Bell*

Opposite bottom: No 1659 was one of two Mark VI Goldliners which were based at Stranraer depot (which is part of the Ulsterbus Tours department), for operation on cross-channel services, and which carried full Eurolines livery. It was photographed in Dumfries en route to Birmingham in June 2000.
Paul Savage

Two of the Mark VI Goldliners were subsequently transferred to Citybus as private hire coaches. Their livery was singularly uninspired, the Ulsterbus blue being replaced with red; fleetnames were omitted altogether. Later, the wave effect was also deleted, as shown on No 1652 picking up passengers outside the Belfast Welcome Centre in Donegall Place. *Paul Savage*

Another of the batch, No 1656, based in Derry, is used almost exclusively on private hire and tours work and has acquired this interesting livery, a compromise between its original Goldline 'wave' styling and the three colour stripe used by the Belfast based touring coach fleet.
John Durey

The choice of vehicle for use on Goldline work ultimately followed the Tours Department, with the acquisition of Irizar-bodied Scanias, although those for Goldline work were on the lower-powered K94 chassis with the InterCentury body built to a comfortable, but slightly lower specification. No 1663 is seen here posed at Foyle Street bus station, Derry, when brand new.
John Durey

Belfast–Dublin Express

One of the 'early winners' of the new Ulsterbus regime was the introduction of an express coach service between Belfast and Dublin, for which a licence was secured, despite railway opposition, in 1989. This was the first daily coach connection between the two capitals since the pioneering services introduced in 1927 by HMS Catherwood, and the rival International Bus Service (SH Weir and AS Baird), later acquired and consolidated by Catherwoods. Catherwood was obliged to withdraw the service prior to the compulsory acquisition of bus operations in Southern Ireland around 1932.

The new service was shared equally between Ulsterbus Express and Bus Éireann *Expressway*. It was the companies' intention to launch the service with a unique marketing brand name and image. However, it proved impossible to identify a name which would be politically neutral and equally meaningful in both Belfast and Dublin, and the service was launched with the prosaic, but factual, title of Belfast–Dublin Express. Later, the Goldline Express image was so successful that it was extended to include the cross-border services, with Bus Éireann applying their equally successful *Expressway* branding.

The first vehicle entrusted to operate the Belfast–Dublin service was No 530, one of four Leyland Tiger coaches with Duple Duple 340 bodies, purchased for the Tours Department in the same year. This photograph shows the coach preparing to leave Belfast during the early weeks of the operation. The coach retains its Ulsterbus Tours livery and carries bold lettering to identify the service. The terminal at Great Victoria Street is in a state of reconstruction, with remnants of the former Great Victoria Street rail station still to be dismantled, but with the Europa Buscentre and multi-storey car park taking shape behind the temporary departure stands.

Paul Savage

BELFAST-DUBLIN
BUS EIREANN
ULSTERBUS
DUBLIN-BELFAST EXPRESS
Leyland
B272 AMG

DUBLIN - BELFAST
BUS EIREANN
BELFAST - DUBLIN EXPRESS
EXCEPT BUSES &
AUTHORISED VEHICLES
IN
Ulsterbus Tours
VAN HOOL
SI 2026

Opposite top: Another Leyland Tiger transferred from the Tours department for use on the Dublin service was No 540, with Wrights Contour coachwork. This view was taken at Hillsborough in the second year of the operation. *Raymond Bell*

Opposite bottom: Very similar lettering was applied to Bus Éireann Van Hool Acron CVH 26 to operate their share of the schedule. It is seen here in November 1989 departing from Great Victoria Street bus station.
Paul Savage

No 1413, one of the Mark III Goldliners was caught by the photographer at Connolly Station, Dublin, during its layover after a journey on the Belfast to Dublin Express in 1993, by which time the use of Goldliner coaches without route branding had become established. The area where the coaches are resting is now much changed and has become the Connolly terminus for the LUAS light rail service.
Raymond Bell

No 1601, a brand new Volvo B10M with Plaxton Premier body is seen calling at Dublin Airport en route to Dublin in August 1996.

John Goan

A spin-off from the Belfast–Dublin route was the introduction of a new, cross country, Goldline Express service 240 from Downpatrick and Newcastle to Newry making direct connections to and from the Dublin service. It is here seen being operated by Mk IV Goldliner No 1592, calling at Castlewellan in April 2000.

John Goan

Airbus

Following the introduction of minibuses on the *Airbus* service between Belfast City Centre and Belfast International Airport at Aldergrove in 1988, a policy decision was taken that the vehicles for the *Airbus* service should be renewed every three years, because of the unusually high mileages achieved by these vehicles. The second generation of *Airbus* vehicles were Mercedes 811D chassis with Wrights 'TS' bodies. These featured the more stylish 'fast front' design developed by Wrights for Ulsterbus, and were also fitted with wheelchair lifts, mounted under a special additional doorway toward the rear of the vehicle, so that the *Airbus* service could become the first fully 'accessible' service in the province. The vehicles were also longer than the Busybuses previously supplied by Mercedes and Wrights, to permit luggage racks to be incorporated within the saloon without reducing the seating capacity.

This photograph, taken in 1991, shows one of the batch, No 1806, at the Europa Buscentre where the platform dedicated to the *Airbus* service had had a short paved projection to improve passenger access. As a result of this photograph being taken, it was accepted that a further modification to the paving would be required to facilitate wheelchair access.

Author

In practice, demand for wheelchair access proved to be minimal, so the next batch were ordered without the wheelchair lifts, one of the previous batch being retained at Great Victoria Street depot in case the wheelchair requirement should arise. No 1811 of this group was taking part in the annual Bus and Coach Rally when it was photographed in April 1993 before entering service.
Richard Whitford

For the next group of *Airbus* vehicles in 1996, Ulsterbus reverted to the Metrorider design, by now being constructed by the Optare company of Leeds. They were built to quite a high specification, with reclining seats and bonded double glazing. No 1818 is depicted at the Aldergrove terminal point in February 2000.
Norman Johnston

The next *Airbus* vehicles comprised Dennis Dart SLF chassis with Wrights 'Crusader' bodywork. These vehicles were all painted with distinctive advertising liveries promoting Easyjet, which by then was the principal airline serving Belfast International (Aldergrove). No 649 is shown here at Great Victoria Street bus park, awaiting its next turn of duty on the demanding motorway run to the airport. *Richard Whitford*

The final group of *Airbus* vehicles within the period covered by this volume were Scania L94UBs with Wright Solar bodywork. By this time, helped by the intensive use of Aldergrove Airport by low-cost, no-frills airlines, patronage of the *Airbus* service had grown to such an extent as to justify the use of full-size vehicles, after a period of fifteen years of operation with midibuses. *Paul Savage*

137

Service Vehicles

For many years it has been bus company practice to retain and modify a 'retired' service bus at each depot to attend at breakdowns, and if necessary to tow the disabled vehicle back to its base. As a result, it is not unusual for the selected vehicles to outlive other buses of the same batch by ten or more years. The companies also retain a range of other commercial vehicles for various purposes, both in their engineering and commercial activities.

This Leyland Leopard with Plaxton Panorama body was a survivor from the earliest days of Ulsterbus. No 584 had been purchased in 1967, at the very outset of the company and was still serving Enniskillen as the depot towing vehicle when photographed in September 1989.
John Goan

Former Ulsterbus Bedford YRQ No 1763 was converted for towing in 1984 and continued to operate for Citybus until 1993. On this occasion, in July 1990 it was attending to a Bristol RE in Donegall Square West, Belfast. Surprisingly its two sisters retained Ulsterbus livery, though not fleetnames, during their years at Citybus.
Paul Savage

This Bedford YLQ, No 1875, was converted into a towing vehicle in 1989 and was still in use at Newtownards depot when photographed in April 1994.
Paul Savage

Several Leyland Leopards of 1975–8 vintage were converted into engineering vehicles; one such is former Ulsterbus No 1935, which has performed this function at Citybus, Short Strand depot since 1993, in full Citybus livery. On this occasion, on the Sydenham By-pass in April 2002 it was towing Daimler Fleetline open-topper No 2863. The combined age of the two vehicles exceeds fifty-five years! *Norman Johnston*

A similar, but slightly younger, Leyland Leopard, No 118, was the engineering vehicle at Omagh, when photographed in the town in June 2001. In common with several of this batch, the attractive ROI registration mark had been transferred as a 'cherished mark' after the vehicle changed its role. Indeed its fleet number was also changed later, to 4118, to release the original for a new luxury coach.

Norman Johnston

The Leopards allocated to engineering/towing duties were shortened by cutting the chassis behind the rear axle; the original rear windows and roof dome were then re-fitted. This view of No 4108 was taken at Magherafelt in May 2003. Note that coach-style wheel trims have been fitted! An earlier view of this vehicle, when in service from Larne depot, appears on page 75 of Buses in Ulster Vol 4, *Ulsterbus, the Heubeck Years*.

Paul Savage

Leyland Leopard No 126 had just been converted for towing duties at Dungannon when it was photographed in June 1998. The livery seems to be a combination of the contemporary, simplified Leyland Tiger livery, with a touch of the Volvo 'Ultra' low floor style at the rear!

John Goan

A more comprehensive recovery service is provided by two purpose-built vehicles which are better equipped for the removal of accident damaged vehicles. Ulsterbus Leyland Roadtrain DXI 2501 was photographed in Bangor in April 1994, resplendent with post-1990 livery and signage. *Raymond Bell*

This Ford flatbed lorry, HXI 2325, is used by the Engineering Department to transport stores and mechanical units between provincial depots and Central Workshops at Duncrue Street. It was photographed in May 1994.
Raymond Bell

Another unit lorry, Iveco HAZ 9145, was still displaying the pre-Translink Ulsterbus signage when it was photographed in December 1997 in Duncrue Street.
Raymond Bell

Typical of the small panel vans operated around Belfast by the Parcellink section of the Commercial Department is Ford Transit BCZ 4743, displaying signage and lettering of the Translink era. The picture was taken outside the Europa Buscentre parcel office in September 1999.
Raymond Bell

Premises

One of the most significant differences in the development of public transport between Northern Ireland and Great Britain during the 1990s was in the realm of public bus station premises. After deregulation of the bus industry in Britain, many long-standing bus stations, whether owned by operating companies or by local councils, were closed and sold off for redevelopment. As a result, the quality of facilities for intending passengers was much reduced. However in Northern Ireland, the strongly market-oriented policy driven by Managing Director Ted Hesketh, ensured that the established Ulsterbus policy of retaining and progressively improving bus station facilities for passengers, not only continued, but accelerated. Indeed from the very basic functional designs of the 1970s, the company now planned and built Buscentres which were highly significant architectural achievements in their local context.

Londonderry bus station was the first to be opened in the new era, in 1988. This is a conventional red brick building incorporating offices for the Area Manager and the Lough Swilly company, as well as passenger facilities for all country bus and express service coach departures. This photo taken in 1995 shows the effort made by local staff to maintain a bright and friendly appearance for customers.
Author

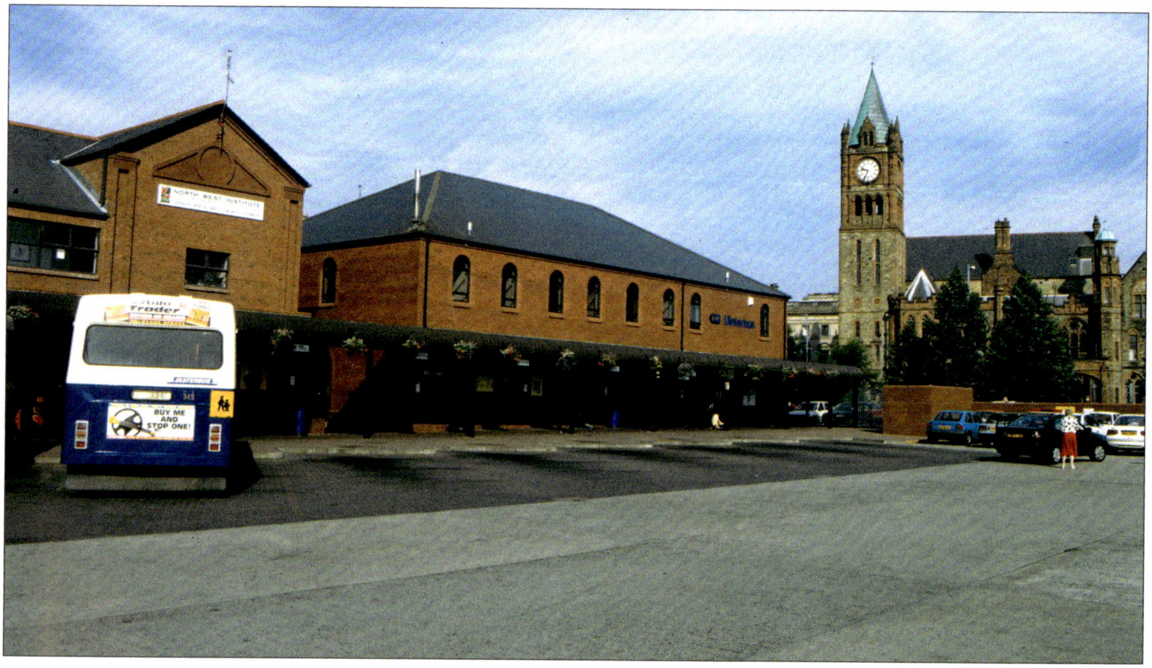
NORTH WEST INSTITUTE
Auto Trader
BUY ME AND STOP ONE!

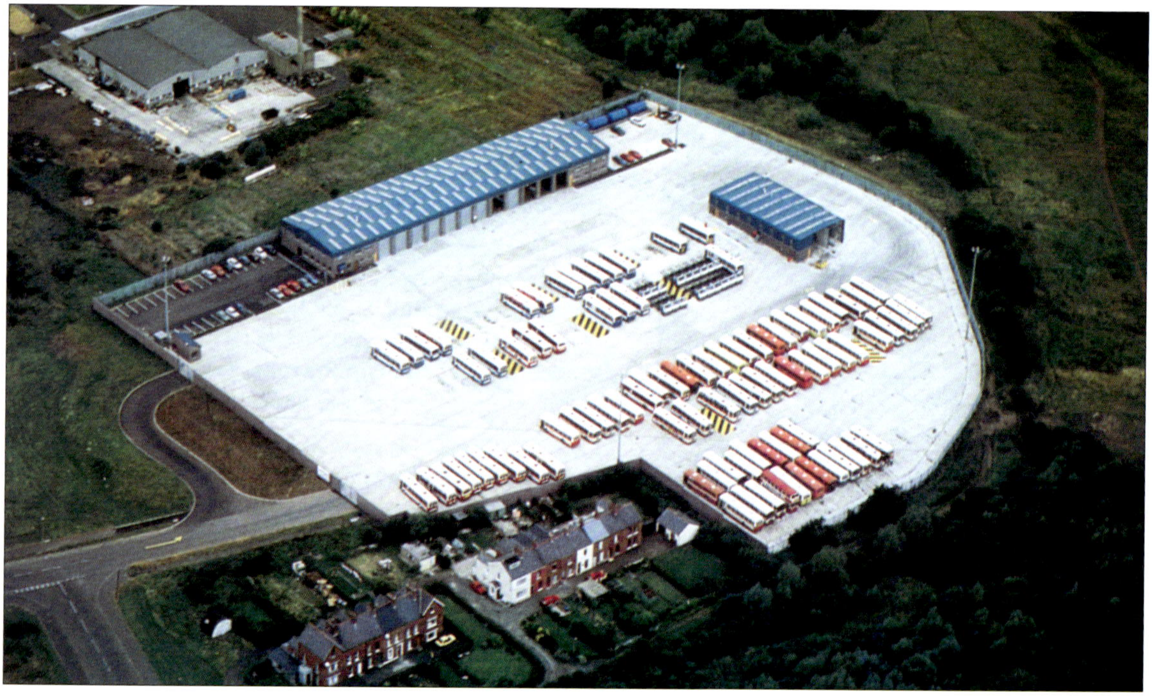

Opposite: Foyle Street, Londonderry with the Guildhall in the background. *Author*

The Europa Buscentre, which replaced the former Great Victoria Street rail and bus stations opened in 1991. Several of the bus photographs elsewhere in this volume demonstrate that the site continued to serve passengers throughout the construction phase. The bus departure stands are aligned facing the passenger facilities, situated on the ground floor below the multi-storey car park. The photograph includes one of the Mark I Goldliner coaches introduced in the same year, and one of the earlier Express type Leyland Tigers, which continued to operate express services until replaced by later batches of Goldliners. *John Goan*

Opposite: Although not a public bus station, the new depot opened at Newtownabbey in 1990 was a major development. The first depot to be built on an entirely new site for many years, it provided operating and maintenance facilities for both Ulsterbus and Citybus fleets serving the greatly expanded North Belfast / Newtonabbey area. In effect, it replaced the former Ulsterbus Smithfield depot which had been destroyed in 1978, as well as the former tram depot at Ardoyne, which finally closed in 1993. This aerial view of the depot at the time of opening shows that the allocation of vehicles was largely of Bristol RELLs. Vehicles in the lower area are reserve fleet vehicles, including some second-hand acquisitions in National red livery, awaiting repainting. *Adrian Thompson, courtesy Ulsterbus*

Left: The Travel Centre at the Europa Buscentre provides much-enhanced facilities for customers and staff over what went before – a portakabin! This high-quality area is the administrative hub for Ulsterbus' extensive tours programme covering the UK and Ireland, as well as much of Europe. Bookings for cross-channel express services, National Express, Scottish Citylink, Eurolines and private hire are also dealt with here.
Translink

Below: This is the main concourse at the Europa Buscentre. A spacious area, with much natural lighting and plenty of seating for waiting passengers, this facility has been visited by numerous bus operators and local government officials from Great Britain to examine the concept and design.
Translink

The enquiry office and waiting area at the rebuilt Newtownards bus station. *Translink*

Right and below: Also completed in 1991, the replacement building on the existing, though slightly enlarged, site at Regent Street, Newtownards bore some resemblance to the Londonderry building.
Translink (right)/Author (below)

Omagh bus station also opened in 1991, again a new building on the original site. Local architect Harry Lynch produced a strikingly modern, yet functional design for this important town centre site. *Translink*

Opposite: The same architect designed the new bus station for Enniskillen, completed in 1993, on the same site as that used by Ulsterbus for the earlier, and barely adequate, depot building in 1971. As in other projects, the interior decoration features artwork which depicts the transport history of the area.

Norman Johnston (top)/Raymond Bell (bottom)

149

A last view of Oxford Street bus station, taken in 1995, shortly before it closed for demolition. *Author*

Although Oxford Street bus station, opened in 1960, had been the most modern of the three bus stations in Belfast to be inherited from Ulster Transport by Ulsterbus, its future was in doubt for many years because of plans to redevelop the old cattle market and adjoining sites. With the establishment of the Laganside Corporation to mastermind redevelopment of the entire Lagan waterside area, the site was earmarked for the flagship development of the Waterfront Hall. Although relocated temporarily on a corner of the original site, the bus station was transferred to a new site across the road within an area known as the McCausland site. Laganside Buscentre, like the Europa Buscentre, uses the ground floor area below a multi-storey car park for its passenger and staff facilities. The new centre opened in 1996. *Translink*

Newry was another town (more recently upgraded to city) which had not had a proper bus station. The Ulsterbus depot in Edward Street contained the usual operational and engineering facilities, but did not cater for the public. Bus departures left from street stops on the Mall, convenient for the traditional shopping area, but recent commercial expansion had taken place along the quays. A site was identified on Soho Island, between the Newry Canal and the Newry River, but this was a long narrow site, hardly suitable for use as a bus station. The solution proposed by local architect JL O'Hagan was to build over the river, thereby linking the old and new shopping areas, as well as retaining the island site for bus movements. The upper photograph taken on the day of the official opening ceremony shows the new building and platform area bathed in wintry sunshine; the lower picture shows the enclosed passenger waiting area bridging the river.

Author (upper)/Translink (lower)

Built on the site of the former railway station, a new bus station, costing almost £1million, was opened in Limavady in the winter of 1997. The six covered departure stands cater for around 400 departures each week and the new building provides a much more pleasant facility for both passengers and staff.
Translink

The little village of Dromara, in Co Down, is home to five Ulsterbus vehicles and six drivers. The building, previously occupied by a bookmaker's shop, was opened on 2 March 1998 to provide a passenger waiting room and staff facilities.
Translink

The bus station in Bangor, long established adjoining the railway station, was a logical target for replacement by Translink, with its strong 'integration' ethos. A temporary site was established in the Abbey Street car park, across the road, while work got under way to demolish both the bus and railway stations and build a replacement. The scheme included a new garage building and enlargement of the bus parking area. This view of the site from Castle Park (below), taken in November 1999, shows the temporary bus departure stands, the old garage and the steelwork for the new station taking shape in the background.

Norman Johnston

The new combined bus and rail station at Bangor opened in March 2001, the modern building providing enhanced facilities for customers. The design of the building was important to Translink and, given Bangor's seaside location on the North Down coast, the architect designed the roof in the form of waves, as can be clearly seen in this evening shot taken shortly after opening.

Translink

On the first day of operation of Bangor's new integrated transport centre a low floor Volvo B10BLE occupies Platform 1. Passengers interchange from the railway platforms by escalator, lift or stairs within the main station building.
Norman Johnston

The former bus office in Magherafelt, a fine listed building on Broad Street, was destroyed by a bomb explosion in 1993. A temporary site was established in a nearby car park, while negotiations proceeded to secure an alternative site for an off-street bus station. In due course, the replacement, a complete Buscentre, was completed and opened in 2002.
Author

Demonstrators

In the process of trying to persuade operators to purchase their latest designs, it is usual for manufacturers to offer demonstration vehicles for testing, in passenger service. It was the practice in Ulsterbus and Citybus to allocate a temporary fleet number, and a new series was started at 2002 in 1992. This series reached 2026 during the period covered by this volume. Many other vehicles were inspected by the companies' senior managers, and in most cases, given test drives by managers and driving instructors, albeit not in passenger service.

Although the companies were not urgently seeking an alternative to the Mercedes for minibus duty, the opportunity was taken to test this Talbot Pullman six-wheeler, one of several designs evolved to try to improve access to vehicles of this size. Despite a lack of destination display, the vehicle was operating a *Busybus* service in Bangor in February 1989.
Paul Savage

Despite appearances, this Mercedes with Wright 'TS' body was never owned or operated by Ulsterbus. Displayed by Wrights and Mercedes at the 1989 Coach and Bus Show at NEC, Birmingham, it carried a livery similar to that which had been applied to the *Airbus* MCW Metroriders delivered in 1988 (see 'Buses in Ulster' Vol 4, p107). The first Wrights-bodied Mercedes for the *Airbus* service were delivered a year later. These differed in having the more streamlined 'fast front'. *Author*

155

By 1991/2 the search was on for the most suitable replacement for the Leyland Tiger, which would shortly cease production. In particular this was an issue for Citybus, given the increasing emphasis being placed upon ease of entry. Several vehicles were tested in March 1992, including this DAF SB220 with Optare Delta bodywork, photographed on the Upper Newtownards Road. It was numbered 2002 for the duration of its stay.

Author

An 'impostor' tested on the Dundonald routes in March 1992 was this Alexander-bodied Dennis Lance photographed at Bloomfield. Although dressed in full livery of SMT of Edinburgh, it did not belong to that operator. It was numbered 2003 while with Citybus.

Author

Scania N113CRB/Plaxton Verde No 2004 leaves Donegall Square West en route to Bloomfield and Dundonald. Although this model failed to find favour, the later L94 low floor chassis is now the favoured type for stage carriage duties. *Raymond Bell*

A Mercedes Benz O405, with Alexander bodywork, paid two visits to Citybus – in November 1992 and again in February 1993. During its first stay, it spent much of its time working on the 16/17/20 group of routes to Dundonald. It is seen here at Donegall Square West, in Belfast city centre. Six rigid and four articulated low floor versions of the O405 were purchased in 2000. *Paul Savage*

Demonstrator Test Results – 1992

Fleet No		2002	2003	2004	2005
Chassis		Leyland Tiger	DAF SB220	Dennis Lance	Scania N113CRB	Mercedes O405
Body		Alexander 'Q'	Optare Delta	Alexander 'PS'	Plaxton Verde	Alexander 'PS'
Seats		51	49	50	47	51
Unladen Weight (Kg)		8800	9900	8450	10003	8980
Engine + bhp		Volvo 180	DAF 218	Cummins 211	Scania 206	Merc-Benz 214
Driver reaction			68.2	77.0	81.2	86.6
Fuel cons (mpg)		7.4	6.0	8.2	6.4	7.4
Hill climb (secs)		259	264	209	203	228
Interior noise level (dB)		72.6 / 70.4 **	68.2 **	73.9	70.0 **	69.4
External noise level (dB)		85.9 / 80.0 **	83.7 **	82.3	81.3 **	84.8

** Encapsulated engine

Source: Citybus Engineering

A couple of years previously, in March 1990, a Duple-bodied Dennis Dart was tried in service at Rathfriland depot, where it is seen having just arrived on service 35 from Newry via Shinn Crossroads. It was allocated fleet number 100 during its stay.
Paul Savage

An unusual visitor to Belfast in July 1992, after a similar visit to Dublin, was this DAF SBR220 with Den Oudsten bodywork, which was examined by management and engineers. For obvious reasons the left-hand drive vehicle was not used in service, although it does seem to have been provided with Citybus fleetnames with that in mind!
Raymond Bell

In March 1993 it was the turn of a Volvo B10B with Northern Counties body to show its paces. No 2006 was photographed at Dundonald (Ulster Hospital) terminus.
Paul Savage

Another, though much less successful, contender was the Iveco TurboCity 50 with Alexander body, No 2007, which operated intermittently on various routes during May 1993.
Paul Savage

This Scania MaxCi with East Lancs body worked the 64 route to Downview during its test period in April 1994. This vehicle was numbered 2008. The photograph includes the futuristic Citybus kiosk at Donegall Square West.
Paul Savage

159

A Volvo B6LE/ Wright Crusader, numbered 2011, was used on *Easibus* services in East Belfast in November 1995. It is seen here arriving at Connswater Shopping Centre, the hub of the *Easibus* network in this part of the city.

Paul Savage

Another vehicle tested on the Downview service was this Optare Excel (No 2012). By January 1997, manufacturers were really pushing the concept of ultra low floor designs.

Raymond Bell

Although the companies had bought the Volvo B10L with Alexander Ultra bodies in 1996, this model did not find great favour, and was soon withdrawn from the market. This Volvo B10BLE with Wright Renown body was offered as a demonstrator in November 1997, and operated in Bangor and Derry, as well as Citybus Short Strand over three months as fleet number 2013. The trial was followed by large orders for this model.
Paul Savage

Alexanders also offered this Volvo B10BLE as a demonstrator in October 1998, by which time the one bus schedule on service 87 to Annadale had become the preferred test route. It carried fleet number 2015, but did not secure orders.
Raymond Bell

Wrights Coachbuilders were investing heavily in research and development of alternative power systems. This battery powered bus, based upon a Dennis Dart chassis, with Wright Crusader body was operated experimentally as a joint Wright/Ulsterbus project between Ballymena and the Ecos Centre during September 2000. No fleet number was carried.

Raymond Bell

By 2000 attention was being focussed on double-deckers. This Dennis Trident, with Alexander ALX400 body, performed for Citybus as No 2019 in December 2000. *Paul Savage*

ECZ 9021, a Scania L94UB with Wright Solar body, arrived on demonstration in May 2000 and was allocated to Larne as No 2021. It stayed for a year and was purchased in May 2001, later becoming No 700. The low floor Scania L94 with Wright Solar body has become the companies' choice for service buses.

Paul Savage

Although almost identical in appearance to the Mark IV Goldliners, this is actually a Volvo B7R with Plaxton Prima body. It spent two months from September 2000 operating on Goldline express services, carrying No 2022. It was caught by the photographer in Lower Abbey Street, Dublin, about to run to Busaras, the central bus station, to begin its return journey to Belfast on service 200.

Paul Savage

Larne depot was also host to another Wrights-bodied demonstration vehicle, this time a Volvo B7L which was allocated fleet number 2023 (GCZ 9023) during its stay. The Volvo B7L features a side mounted engine on the nearside of the chassis which results in an unusual, some say claustrophobic, interior arrangement at the rear of the vehicle. No orders followed from No 2023's visit.

Paul Savage

163

Around the same time this Volvo with Plaxton President bodywork performed on the Four Winds service, complete with 'Go' logo. The photo was taken in Bedford Street in December 2000. The contortions some motorists will adopt to get parked on bus stops are well illustrated!

Paul Savage

Another development vehicle produced by Wrights was the Electrocity, which operated on the Ballymena town service during June 2002, bearing No 2025. This hybrid vehicle combined a small diesel engine with a battery pack, one of several good ideas which have been developed by the transport industry over the last ten to twenty years, yet few of the concepts have achieved production volumes.

Raymond Bell

Company people

Citybus and Ulsterbus staff celebrate the launch of the first 'Cityliner' buses in 1991.
Ulsterbus

Board members of NITHCo and Ulsterbus, with Managers and District Council guests after the opening of Enniskillen Buscentre in 1993. Included, from left are: Fred Penhaligon (Chartermark), Gerry Burns (Fermanagh DC), Tom Andrews, Bobby Wilson, Margaret Elliott, Jim Irvine (NITHCo), Andy Watt, Trevor Griffiths, Ian Doherty, Tom McClintock, Myles Humphries (NIR), Trevor Pearson (DoE), Bertie Kerr (Chairman, Fermanagh DC), Ted Hesketh, Bill Bradshaw (Chairman), Helen Roulston, Bob Gourley, Don Price (NIR), Billy Telford, Amanda Carson, Mal McGreevy, Mrs Bradshaw, Alan Mercer, Harry McGee, Frank Clegg, Raymond Gault, Brian Delaney. *Ulsterbus*

The new Buscentre at Newry was officially opened by Lord Dubs on 19 November 1999. He is seen here, cutting a specially-commissioned Goldliner cake, accompanied by members of staff and management including District Manager Aidan Faloona (left), Ted Hesketh, Paul Haughey, Joan Smyth, Paul McCourt, Anastasia O'Hare, Mark Bronte, Hilary Sterritt, David Cowan, Jimmy Hanley, Maria Kennedy, Joe Murphy and Willie Mulholland. *Translink*

Amanda Watson, from Craigavon depot, won the Bus Driver of the Year competition in 1999, for the second time. Bobby Carson, full-time officer of the GMB, presents Amanda with the GMB Union trophy. *Translink*

Right: Translink won the Commission for Integrated Transport Customer Services Award at the 2002 Bus Industry Awards. Pictured here (front to back) are Michelle McClelland and Mark Peden (drivers at Great Victoria Street), Ted Hesketh and Philip O'Neill (Director of Operations). *Translink*

Ulsterbus and Citybus Managers 1988–2003

Managing Director (Ulsterbus & Citybus)
Ted Hesketh 1988–1995

Managing Director – Operations (Translink)
Ted Hesketh 1995–2003

Chief Engineer (Ulsterbus)
Ken Middleton 1970–1991

Chief Engineer (Citybus)
Tom Campbell 1973–1991

Chief Engineer (Ulsterbus & Citybus)
Mal McGreevy 1991–1996

Engineering Executive (Translink)
Mal McGreevy 1996– +

Works Manager (U)
Mal McGreevy 1988–1991
Brian McMullen 1991–1998
Sam Johnston 1998– +

Technical & Garage Engineering Manager (U)
Eric Fiddament 1969–1997

Engineering Manager (Citybus)
James Erwin 1991–1996

Financial Controller (U & C)
Brian Delaney 1990–1996

Finance Executive (Translink)
Brian Delaney 1996–1999
Stephen Armstrong 1999– +

Company Secretary (U&C)
Brian Lyle 1988–1990
Gareth Kirk 1990–1991

Commercial Manager (Ulsterbus)
Brian Carson 1988–1991
Sam Dowling 1991–1992
Gareth Kirk 1992–1996
David Leathem 1996– +

Business Development Manager (U&C)
Tom Andrews 1991–1996

Transport Development Manager
Irvine Lavery 1998– +

Staff Officer (U&C)
Sam Thompson 1966–1991

Head of Human Resources (U&C)
Alan Mercer 1990–1996

Human Resources Executive (Translink)
Alan Mercer 1996– +

Inspector General (U&C)
Irvine Millar 1988–2001

Belfast Operational Review Manager
Frank Clegg 1999–2001

Network Technical Support Manager
Frank Clegg 2001– +

Chief Driving Instructor/Training Manager
Pat Deehan 1968–1990
Maurice Kennedy 1990–1993
Trevor Dixon 1993– +

Operations Executive (Translink)
Andy Watt 1988– 2002
Philip O'Neill 2002– +

Area Managers:

Central/Belfast Area
Tom Andrews 1983–1990
(Ulsterbus & Citybus) Frank Clegg 1990–1999
Philip O'Neill 1999–2002
Billy Gilpin 2002– +

Southern Area (U)
Bobby Wilson 1985–1993
Maurice Kennedy 1993–1997
David Cowan 1997– +

Northern Area (U)
Sam Dowling 1987–1991
Billy Telford 1992– +

Western Area (U) (Area merged 1996)
Andy Watt 1989–1996

Depot Managers:

Antrim
Dennis Kennedy 1988–1990
Eleanor Ramsay 1990–2001
Martin Lundy 2001– +

Ardoyne (C) (Depot closed 1993)
Eddie Rothwell 1976–1989
Frank Ward 1990–1993

Armagh
John J Campbell	1984–1994
Greg McLaughlin	1994– +

Ballymena
Tony Wylie	1984–2005

Bangor
Billy Telford	1982–1991
Eugene O'Callaghan	1991–1996
David Leathem	1996
Richard Hudson	1997
William McGookin	1998– +

Coleraine
Ricky McArthur	1986–1993
Conor O'Cleary	1993–2003
Jonathan Miller	2003– +

Craigavon
Randall Roderick	1987– +

Downpatrick
Hugh Scott	1988–2000
Garry Mawhinney	2000– +

Dungannon
John Kidd	1982– +

Enniskillen
Raymond Gault	1988–1999
Martin Lundy	1999–2001
Sam Todd	2003– +

Falls (C)
Billy Hamilton	1975–1989
Gerry Carson	1989–2002
Damien Bannon	2002– +

Great Victoria Street/Europa (U)
Richard Hudson	1989–1997
Aidan Faloona	1997–1998
Richard Hudson	1998– +

Larne
Conor O'Cleary	1982–1993
William Patton	1993– +

Lisburn
Bobby Campbell	1987–1990
Bob Pauley	1990–1992
John Lundy	1992– +

Londonderry
David Leathem	1988–1994
Tony McDaid	1994–2004

Derry City
Alan Young	1996–2000

Magherafelt
Jack McAllister	1989–1994
Terry Butler	1994–2002
Sean Falls	2002– +

Newcastle
Eileen Starkey	1988–1998
Charlie McGrath	1998–2003

Newry
PJ Darby	1988–1995
David Leathem	1996
Eugene O'Callaghan	1996–1998
Aidan Faloona	1998–2005

Newtownabbey (U&C)
Maurice Kennedy	1990–1993
Gerry Mullen	1993– +

Newtownards
Billy Brown	1982–1990
Dennis Kennedy	1990–2005

Omagh
Brian McClean	1982–1989
PJ McGowan	1989–2000
Alan Young	2000– +

Oxford Street/Laganside
Paddy Moss	1988–2005

Short Strand (C)
Roy Sloan	1987– +

+ indicates that these managers' tenure of office continued beyond the period covered by this volume.

(Translink) indicates appointments of the Northern Ireland Transport Holding Company.

Space has not permitted inclusion of managers who covered additional or alternative positions in depots or areas on a temporary basis.

Fleet list

The fleet list is in four main parts. The first contains a summary, in chronological order, of the original batches from which vehicles existed at the beginning of 1989. Buses built new for Ulsterbus, Citybus and Flexibus between 1989 and 2003 are summarised in the second section, again in chronological order. These tables indicate the period during which vehicles were withdrawn from passenger service under normal circumstances. The actual withdrawal dates for individual vehicles (up to 2003) are listed in the fourth section. The third table lists pre-owned vehicles acquired by the comapnies between 1989 and 2003, mostly as replacements for vehicles lost in civil disturbances. Withdrawal dates, where relevant, for individual vehicles are listed. In all cases, these refer to withdrawal from normal passenger service, not sale or disposal, as withdrawn vehicles have often been retained in reserve, or broken up for spares. Finally, there are listings of vehicles re-numbered or re-registered and vehicles used for towing or driver training after normal withdrawal.

PSV Circle codes to describe bodywork and seating are used in the column headed 'Seats' and are explained as follows:

B	Bus seating	F	Front or forward entrance
C	Coach seating	R	Rear entrance
DP	Dual-purpose (coach seating in bus body)	RD	Rear entrance with door
H	High-bridge double-decker	D	Dual doorway (front entrance/centre exit)
O	Open-top double-decker	T	Toilet
A	Articulated		

(Seating of double-deckers is quoted as upper deck followed by lower deck.)

Suffixes used in the lists:

a	withdrawn due to accident	(B)	Belfast factory
f	withdrawn with accidental fire damage	(F)	Falkirk factory
m	withdrawn due to malicious damage/destruction	C	delivered new to/acquired for Citybus
p	preserved	F	delivered new to/acquired for Flexibus
r	retained as garage towing vehicle	R	funded by Rural Transport Fund for community transport schemes. Maintained by Translink.
s	sold to another operator		
t	retained as driver training vehicle	U	delivered new to/acquired for Ulsterbus
n.o.	not operated	*	denotes inter-company transfers at various times

(1) Vehicles built new for Ulsterbus, Citybus and Flexibus before 1989

This list shows complete batches. Vehicles extant in 1989 and subsequently withdrawn are shown in the withdrawal list which follows.

Fleet No	Reg No	Co	Built	Chassis type	Body type	Seats	Wdn
911–21/3	COI 911–21/3	U	1971	Leyland Atlantean PDR2/1	Alexander (B)	H48/37F [1]	1986–90
922/4–50	COI 922/4–50	U	1972–73	Leyland Atlantean PDR2/1	Alexander (B)	H48/37F [1,2]	1986–90
2853–72	EOI 4853–72	C	1972–73	Daimler Fleetline CRG6-33	Alexander (B)	H46/31D [3]	1989
1703–99	HOI 1703–99	U	1974–75	Bedford YRQ	Alexander (B)	B45F	1982–89
1800	HOI 800	U	1975	Bedford YRQ	Alexander (B)	B45F	1989
1901–08	HOI 1901–08	U	1975	Leyland Leopard PSU3C/4R	Alexander (B)	C49F	1989
1913–35	HOI 2913–35	U	1975	Leyland Leopard PSU3C/4R	Alexander (B)	DP49F	1989–90
2001–28	JOI 3001–28	U	1975	Bristol RELL6G	Alexander (B)	B44D	1989–90
2029–40	JOI 3029–40	U	1975	Bristol RELL6G	Alexander (B)	B50F	1989–91
1936–65	KOI 9936–65	U	1976	Leyland Leopard PSU3C/4R	Alexander (B)	DP49F	1990–91
1833–80	LOI 1833–80	U	1976–77	Bedford YLQ	Alexander (B)	B45F	1989
2041–80	LOI 2041–80	C	1976–77	Bristol RELL6G	Alexander (B)	B32D [4]	1991
2081–120	MOI 8081–120	C	1976–77	Bristol RELL6G	Alexander (B)	B32D [4]	1991
2121–35	MOI 2121–35	U	1976–77	Bristol RELL6G	Alexander (B)	B44D	1990–92

Fleet No	Reg No	Co	Built	Chassis type	Body type	Seats	Wdn
1966–89	NOI 1966–89	U	1977	Leyland Leopard PSU3D/4R [6]	Alexander (B)	DP49F	1990–94
1990–95	NOI 1990–95	U	1977–78	Leyland Leopard PSU3E/4R	Duple Dominant II	C49F	1991–92
2136–70	POI 2136–70	C	1977	Bristol RELL6G	Alexander (B)	B32D [4]	1991
2171–210	POI 2171–210	U*	1977–78	Bristol RELL6G	Alexander (B)	B52F [8]	1995–97
2211–30	ROI 2211–30	C	1978	Bristol RELL6G	Alexander (B)	B32D [4]	1992
105–50	ROI 105–50	U	1978	Leyland Leopard PSU3E/4R	Alexander (B)	DP49F [22]	1997–2006
2231–70	ROI 2231–70	U*	1978–79	Bristol RELL6G	Alexander (B)	B52F [8]	1998–2000
1591	SOI 3591	U	1978	Leyland Leopard PSU3A/4R	Alexander (B)	B53F	1989
151–56	TOI 151–56	U	1979	Leyland Leopard PSU3E/4R	Duple Dominant I	C53F	1990
1996–99	TOI 1996–99	U	1979	Leyland Leopard PSU3E/4R	Duple Dominant II	C49F	1992
2271–305	TOI 2271–305	U*	1979	Bristol RELL6G	Alexander (B)	B52F [8]	1999–2000
2306–20	TOI 2306–20	C*	1979	Bristol RELL6G	Alexander (B)	B50F [9]	1994–2000
2321–60	UOI 2321–60	C	1979–80	Bristol RELL6G	Alexander (B)	B32D [4,7]	1993–96
2361–400	UOI 2361–400	U*	1979–80	Bristol RELL6G	Alexander (B)	B52F [8]	1999–2003
157–70	UOI 9157–70	U	1980	Leyland Leopard PSU3E/4R	Alexander (B)	DP49F	2003–06
171–206	VOI 171–206	U	1980	Leyland Leopard PSU3E/4R	Alexander (B)	DP49F [5]	2000–2006
2401–30	VOI 8401–30	C	1980–81	Bristol RELL6G	Alexander (B)	B32D [4]	1994–96
2431–60	WOI 2431–60	U*	1980–82	Bristol RELL6G	Alexander (B)	B52F [8]	1991–2001
207–26	WOI 2207–26	U	1981	Leyland Leopard PSU3E/4R	Alexander (B)	B53F	2006
227–56	WOI 2227–56	U	1981	Leyland Leopard PSU3E/4R	Alexander (B)	DP49F [5]	2006
557–60	WOI 2257–60	U	1981	Leyland Leopard PSU3E/4R	Plaxton Supreme	C53F	1994–96
3001/5	WOI 3001/5	U*	1981	Leyland B21	Alexander (B)	B53F	1991
3002–4	WOI 3002–4	C	1981–82	Leyland B21	Alexander (B)	B--F [20]	1991
561–64	XOI 561–64	C	1981	Leyland Leopard PSU3E/4R	Plaxton Supreme	C49F	1996–97
300–09	XOI 2300–09	U	1981–82	Leyland Leopard PSU3E/4R	Alexander (B)	B53F	2006
2461–80	WOI 8461–80	C	1981–82	Bristol RELL6G	Alexander (B)	B39F [10]	1997–2000
2481–530	XOI 2481–530	C	1982–84	Bristol RELL6G	Alexander (B)	B39F [10]	1997–2004
3000	WOI 607	U	1982	Leyland B21	Alexander (B)	B45D	1991
258	XOI 2258	U	1982	Leyland Leopard PSU3E/4R	Wright TT	DP53F	2006
260–79	YOI 2260–79	U	1982	Leyland Leopard PSU3G/4R	Alexander (B)	DP49F	2006
280–99	AXI 280–99	U	1982	Leyland Leopard PSU3G/4R	Alexander (B)	B53F	2006
259	AXI 2259	U	1982	Leyland Leopard PSU3E/4R	Wright Royal	C53F	1999
310–19	AXI 310–19	U	1982	Leyland Leopard PSU3F/4R	Alexander (B)	B53F	2006
2531–60	AXI 2531–60	C	1983–86	Bristol RELL6G	Alexander (B)	B39F [10]	2003–04
320–39	BXI 320–39	U	1983–84	Leyland Leopard PSU3F/4R	Alexander (B)	DP49F	2006
2581–600	BXI 2581–600	U	1982–83	Bristol RELL6G	Alexander (B)	B52F [8]	2003–04
551–54	BXI 5551–54	U	1983	Leyland Tiger TRCTL11/3R	Duple Caribbean	C51F	1999
555–56	CXI 1555–56	U	1983	Leyland Tiger TRCTL11/3R	Duple Dominant IV	C53F	1995–99
2561–80	BXI 2561–80	C	1983–85	Bristol RELL6G	Alexander (B)	B52F	2003–04
1	DXI 9001	F	1984	Mercedes 609D	Reeve Burgess	C19F	1996
340	DXI 3340	U	1984	Leyland Tiger TRCTL11/2R	Alexander (B) 'N'	DP53F	2006
341–59	DXI 3341–59	U	1984	Leyland Tiger TRBTL11/2RP	Alexander (B) 'N'	DP53F	2006–
360–69	DXI 3360–69	U*	1984	Leyland Tiger TRBTL11/2RP	Alexander (B) 'N'	C53F [11]	2006–
370	DXI 3370	U	1984	Leyland Tiger TRBLXCT/2RP	Alexander (B) 'N'	DP53F	2006
371–79	DXI 3371–79	U	1984	Leyland Tiger TRBTL11/2RP	Alexander (B) 'N'	DP53F	2006–
541–44	EXI 5541–44	U*	1984–85	Leyland Tiger TRCTL11/3RZ	Wright Contour	C57F	1999
545–48	EXI 5545–48	U	1984	Leyland Tiger TRCTL11/2RZ	Duple Laser I	C49F	1995–1997
549–50	EXI 5549–50	U	1984	Leyland Tiger TRCTL11/3RZ	Duple Caribbean	C51F [12]	1999
380–88	FXI 380–88	U	1984	Leyland Tiger TRBTL11/2RP	Alexander (B) 'N'	DP53F	2006–
2–3	EXI 9002–03	F	1985	Mercedes 609D	PMT	C19F	1998
4	GXI 5004	F	1985	Talbot Express	Wright	C12F	1991
5	GXI 5005	F	1985	Renault Traffic Master	Wright	C13F	1994
6	GXI 5006	F	1985	Mercedes 307D	Wright	C12F	1997
7	HXI 4007	F	1985	Mercedes 608D	Ulsterbus	C19F	1996
389–419	FXI 389–419	U	1985	Leyland Tiger TRBTL11/2RP	Alexander (B) 'N'	DP53F	2006–

Fleet No	Reg No	Co	Built	Chassis type	Body type	Seats	Wdn
420–54	GXI 420–54	U	1985	Leyland Tiger TRBTL11/2RP	Alexander (B) 'N'	DP53F	1986–
537–38	GXI 537–38	U	1985	Leyland Tiger TRCTL11/2RZ	Wright Contour	C49F	1998–99
539	GXI 539	U	1985	Leyland Tiger TRCTL11/3RP	Duple Laser II	C53F	1996
540	B272 AMG	U	1985	Leyland Tiger TRCTL11/3RH	Wright Contour	C53F [22]	1991
8–9	HXI 6008–09	F	1986	Mercedes 608D	Ulsterbus	C19F	1996–99
10	HXI 6010	F	1986	Renault Traffic Master	Ulsterbus	C13F	1995
11–12	IXI 1111–12	F	1986	Mercedes 608D	Ulsterbus	C19F	1996
13–14	IXI 3113–14	F	1986	Mercedes 608D	Ulsterbus	C19F	1996–97
17–20	IXI 7017–20	F	1986	Iveco 60.10V	Ulsterbus	C19F	1989–91
23–25	JXI 223–25	F	1986	Mercedes 609D	Ulsterbus	C19F	1996–97
536	IXI 1536	U	1986	Leyland Tiger TRCTL11/3RZ	Duple 320	C55F	2000
600	KXI 600	U*	1987	Volvo B9M	Plaxton Paramount	C39F	2005
455–59	GXI 455–59	U	1986	Leyland Tiger TRBTL11/2RP	Alexander (B) 'N'	DP53F	2006–
460–69	HXI 460–69	U	1986	Leyland Tiger TRBTL11/2RP	Alexander (B) 'N'	C53F [13]	–
470–79	HXI 470–79	U	1986	Leyland Tiger TRBTL11/2RP	Alexander (B) 'N'	DP53F	–
480–99	IXI 1480–99	U	1986	Leyland Tiger TRBTL11/2RP	Alexander (B) 'N'	DP53F	–
1000–09	IXI 1000–09	U	1986	Leyland Tiger TRBTL11/2RP	Alexander (B) 'N'	DP53F	–
1010–18	JXI 1010–18	U	1986	Leyland Tiger TRBTL11/2RP	Alexander (B) 'N'	DP53F	–
3006–10	HXI 3006–10	C	1985–86	Leyland Lynx LX563	Alexander (B) 'N'	B--F [21]	1991
3011–12	HXI 3011–12	U*	1986	Leyland Lynx LX563TL11	Alexander (B) 'N'	B53F	1991
15–16	IXI 7015–16	F	1987	Mercedes 608D	Ulsterbus (tail lift)	C18F	2000–03
21–22	JXI 221–22	F	1987	Renault Traffic Master	Ulsterbus	C13F	1997
26	JXI 226	F	1987	Mercedes 609D	Ulsterbus (tail lift)	C18F	2003
27–30	KXI 1027–30	F	1987	Mercedes 609D	Ulsterbus	C19F	2000
32	LXI 1032	F	1987	Mercedes 609D	Ulsterbus	C19F	–
534–35	JXI 534–35	U	1987	Leyland Tiger TRCTL11/3RZ	Duple 340	C53F [14]	–
1019–39	JXI 1019–39	U	1987	Leyland Tiger TRBTL11/2RP	Alexander (B) 'N'	DP53F	–
1040–59	KXI 1040–59	U	1987	Leyland Tiger TRBTL11/2RP	Alexander (B) 'N'	B53F	–
1060–68	KXI 1060–68	U	1987	Leyland Tiger TRBTL11/2RP	Alexander (B) 'N'	DP53F	–
1069–79	KXI 2069–79	U	1987	Leyland Tiger TRBTL11/2RP	Alexander (B) 'N'	DP53F	–
1080–99	KXI 2080–99	U	1987	Leyland Tiger TRBTL11/2RP	Alexander (B) 'N'	B53F	–
1100–14	LXI 1100–14	U	1987	Leyland Tiger TRBTL11/2RP	Alexander (B) 'N'	DP53F	–
801–04	KXI 7801–04	U	1987	Mercedes 609D	Ulsterbus	B19F [15]	1996–2000
33–35	LXI 1033–35	F	1988	Mercedes 609D	Ulsterbus	C19F	1997
36–37	LXI 1036–37	F	1988	Mercedes 609D	Citybus	C19F	1997–2002
805–08	LXI 6805–08	U*	1988	Mercedes 609D	Ulsterbus	B19F [12]	1996–97
809–10	LXI 6809–10	U*	1988	Mercedes 609D	Citybus	B19F [17]	2000
1115–29	LXI 1115–29	U	1987–88	Leyland Tiger TRBTL11/2RP	Alexander (B) 'N'	B53F	–
1130–39	LXI 1130–39	U	1988	Leyland Tiger TRBTL11/2RP	Alexander (B) 'N'	C53F [16]	–
1801–04	LXI 4801–04	U*	1988	MCW MF150/50	MCW Metrorider	C21F	1992–96
1140–54	LXI 7140–54	U	1988	Leyland Tiger TRBTL11/2RP	Alexander (B) 'N'	DP53F	–
1155–79	MXI 3155–79	U	1988	Leyland Tiger TRBTL11/2RP	Alexander (B) 'N'	B53F	–
811–14	MXI 3811–14	U	1988	Mercedes 609D	Ulsterbus	B19F [18]	1996–2000
815–22	NXI 815–22	U*	1988	Mercedes 609D	Ulsterbus	B19F [19]	1996–2000
1180–99	NXI 1180–99	U	1988	Leyland Tiger TRBTL11/2RP	Alexander (B) 'N'	B53F	–
1200–09	NXI 1200–09	U	1988	Leyland Tiger TRBTL11/2RP	Alexander (B) 'N'	B48F	–

[1] Some were later increased to H48/39F.
[2] Nos 940–50 were originally H48/35F.
[3] No 2857 H43/37F; No 2863 rebuilt to O45/35F in 1991.
[4] Some were subsequently reseated to B35D, B40D or B43D.
[5] Nos 189 and 248 were reseated, No 187 to B63F in 1996 and No 248 to B62F in 1997
[6] Nos 1981–89 were classified PSU3E/4R.
[7] No 2338 was modified to B43F, with centre door sealed, in 1996.
[8] Some were subsequently reseated to B51F.
[9] Reseated to B52F in 1982; Nos 2306–15 subsequently reseated to B51F in 1990.
[10] Some were reseated to B45F in 1989
[11] Nos 360/2–7 were reseated B53F in 1988, No 361 was reseated B34D + wheelchair lift in 1991, Nos 368–9 were reseated B62F in 1993–4.
[12] Nos 549–50 were reseated C53F in 1987.
[13] Nos 460/3 were reseated B53F in 1988.
[14] Nos 534–35 were convertible to C57F.
[15] Nos 801–3 were reseated B24F in 1994–95.
[16] Nos 1130/1/3–9 were reseated B62F in 1993–4.
[17] Nos 806 and 810 were reseated B24F in 1994/5.
[18] No 814 was reseated B24F in 1995.
[19] Nos 815/6/8/20 were reseated B24F, 1993–96.
[20] No 3002 reseated to B42F and No 3006 to B46F, both in 1990.
[21] Nos 3007–10 reseated to B38F in 1987.
[22] No 109 re-reg'd WAZ 5652, No 540 re-reg'd RXI 5540

(2) Vehicles built new for Ulsterbus, Citybus and Flexibus 1989–2003

Fleet No	Reg No	Co.	Built	Chassis type	Body type	Seats	Wdn
2601–10	LXI 6601–10	C*	1988	Leyland Tiger TRBLXB/2RP	Alexander (B) 'N'	B43F	2001–
1210–49	NXI 4210–49	U	1988–89	Leyland Tiger TRBTL11/2RP	Alexander (B) 'N'	DP53F	–
1250–59	OXI 1250–59	U	1989–90	Leyland Tiger TRBTL11/2RP	Alexander (B) 'N'	DP53F	–
1260–99	OXI 1260–99	U	1989–90	Leyland Tiger TRBTL11/2RP	Alexander (B) 'N'	B53F	–
38–41	NXI 6938–41	F*	1989	Mercedes 811D	Ulsterbus conv.	C19F	2000
2611–35	NXI 4611–35	C*	1988–89	Leyland Tiger TRBLXB/2RP	Alexander (B) 'N'	B43F	–
1300–20	PXI 1300–20	U	1990	Leyland Tiger TR2R56V16Z4	Alexander (B) 'N'	DP53F	–
823–62	NXI 6823–62	U*	1989	Mercedes 709D	Wright 'TS'	B23/25F	2000–06
530–33	OXI 530–33	U	1989	Leyland Tiger TRCTL11/3ARZ4	Duple 340	C55F[1]	2001–04
1321	RXI 3321	U	1990	Leyland Tiger TR2R56V16Z4	Alexander (B) 'Q'	DP53F	–
1322–39	RXI 3322–39	U	1990	Leyland Tiger TR2R56V16Z4	Alexander (B) 'N'	DP53F	–
514–29	PXI 5514–29	U	1990	Leyland Tiger TRCTL11/3ARZ4	Alexander (B) 'TE'	C53F	2002–
677–80	SXI 1677–80	U	1990	DAF MB230DKFL	Plaxton Paramount	C53F[2]	2002–06
1805–09	SXI 2805–09	U*	1990	Mercedes 811D	Wright 'TS'	C23FL	2002–05
863–82	TXI 7863–82	U*	1991–2	Mercedes 709D	Wright 'TS'	B25F	2003–06
672–676	UXI 1672–76	U	1991	DAF MB230DKFL	Plaxton Paramount	C53F[2]	2003–06
2636–60	SXI 2636–60	C*	1991	Leyland Tiger TR2R56V16Z4	Alexander (B) 'Q'	B51F	–
1340–59	TXI 1340–59	U	1991	Leyland Tiger TR2R56V16Z4	Alexander (B) 'Q'	C49F	–
1360–79	UXI 1360–79	U	1991–2	Leyland Tiger TR2R56V16Z4	Alexander (B) 'Q'	DP53F	–
2661–64	VXI 2661–64	C	1991	Leyland Tiger TR2R56V16Z4	Alexander (B) 'Q'	B38F[3]	–
2665–80	VXI 2665–80	C	1991	Leyland Tiger TR2R56V16Z4	Alexander (B) 'Q'	B51F	–
1380–99	WXI 4380–99	U	1992	Leyland Tiger TR2R56V16Z4	Alexander (B) 'Q'	DP53F	–
1400–07	WXI 1400–07	C*	1992	Leyland Tiger TR2R62V16Z4	Alexander (B) 'Q'	C53F	–
1408–32	WXI 4408–32	U	1992	Leyland Tiger TR2R62V16Z4	Wright Endeavour	C53F	–
1433–49	XXI 1433–49	U	1992	Leyland Tiger TR2R62V16Z4	Alexander (B) 'Q'	B64F	–
1450–54	WXI 4450–54	U	1992	Leyland Tiger TR2R56V16Z4	Alexander (B) 'Q'	DP53F	–
1455–79	YXI 1455–79	C	1992–3	Leyland Tiger TR2R56V16Z4	Alexander (B) 'Q'	DP51F	–
1480–82	YXI 1480–82	C*	1992	Leyland Tiger TR2R56V16Z4	Alexander (B) 'Q'	C49F	–
1483–500	YXI 5483–500	U	1993	Leyland Tiger TR2R56V16Z4	Alexander (B) 'Q'	DP53F	–
670–71	AAZ 1670–71	U	1993	DAF MB230DKFL	Plaxton Paramount	C49FT	–
883–92	AAZ 8883–92	U	1993	Mercedes 709D	Wright 'TS'	B25F	2003–05
1810–13	AAZ 6810–13	U*	1993	Mercedes 811D	Wright 'TS'	C24F[4]	2005
504–5	DAZ 5504–5	U	1994	Volvo B10M	Plaxton Excalibur	C47FT	–
601	CAZ 6641	U	1994	Dennis Dart	Wright Handybus	B39F	2005
602–23	CAZ 6602–23	U	1994	Dennis Dart	Wright Handybus	B39F	2005–06
624	CAZ 6624	C	1994	Dennis Dart	Wright Handybus	B34F	2005
625–40	CAZ 6625–40	C	1994	Dennis Dart	Wright Handybus	B39F	2005–06
3000–01	DAZ 3000–01	C*	1994	Volvo B10MA	Van Hool	AC79D	–
1501–50	DAZ 1501–50	U	1994	Volvo B10M-60	Alexander (B) 'Q'	B65F	–
1551–73	DAZ 1551–73	U*	1994	Volvo B10M-62	Plaxton Premier 320	C53F	–
1574–600	EAZ 5574–600	U	1994–5	Volvo B10M-62	Plaxton Premier 320	C53F	–
1814	HAZ 5814	U	1995	Mercedes 811D	Wright 'TS'	B26F	–
506–10	GAZ 5506–10	U	1995	Volvo B10M–62	Plaxton Excalibur	C49FT	–
43/5–8	IAZ 6043/5–8	F	1995	Renault Master T35D	Oughtred & Harrison	B12F	–
511–12	JAZ 5511–12	U	1996	Volvo B10M-49	Caetano Algarve II	C34FT[5]	–
687–90	JAZ 6687–90	U	1996	Volvo B10M–62	Plaxton Excalibur	C49FT	–
893–922	JAZ 3893–922	U*	1996	Mercedes 711D	Alexander (B)	B25F	–
1601–30	JAZ 1601–30	U	1996	Volvo B10M-62	Plaxton Premier 320	C53F	–
2701–50	LAZ 2701–50	C	1996–7	Volvo B10L	Alexander (B) Ultra	B44F	–

Fleet No	Reg No	Co.	Built	Chassis type	Body type	Seats	Wdn
2751–60	LAZ 2751–60	U	1996	Volvo B10L	Alexander (B) Ultra	B44F	–
2900	JAZ 5900	U	1996	Gentrac Roadtrain		64	–
3002–03	JAZ 3002–03	U	1996	Volvo B10MA	Van Hool Alizee	AC71D	–
1815–18	JAZ 1815–18	U*	1996	Optare Metrorider	Optare	DP24F	2005
641–2	LAZ 7641–2	C*	1997	Dennis Dart SLF	Wright Crusader	B25F	–
643–7	YAZ 8643–7	U*	1999	Dennis Dart SLF	Wright Crusader	B25F	–
691–4	ACZ 6691–4	U	1999	Volvo B10M–62	Plaxton Excalibur	C49FT	–
1631–50	BCZ 1631–50	U	1999	Volvo B10M–62	Plaxton Excalibur	C53F	–
1651–60	BCZ 1651–60	U	1999	Volvo B10M–62	Plaxton Excalibur	C49FT	–
2001	BCZ 2001	C*	1999	Ayats	Ayats Bravo I	C57/18CT	–
2762–806	BCZ 2762–806	C*	1999	Volvo B10BLE	Wright Renown	B45F	–
67–72	CCZ 6067–72	R	1999–2000	Mercedes 410D Sprinter	NuTrack	B16F	–
73–7	CCZ 6073–7	R	1999–2000	Renault Master	NuTrack	B12F	–
2807–51	CCZ 8807–51	U*	1999–2000	Volvo B10BLE	Wright Renown	B45F	–
2100–5	DCZ 2100–5	C	2000	Mercedes O405N	Mercedes	B44F	–
3100–3	DCZ 3100–3	C	2000	Mercedes O405GN	Mercedes	AB59D	–
1819–28	DCZ 4819–28	U	2000	Optare Solo M850	Optare	B26F	–
648–51	DCZ 7648–51	U	2000	Dennis Dart SLF	Wright Crusader	DP25F	–
78–86	ECZ 7078–86	R	2000–02	Renault Master	NuTrack	B12F	–
695–9	ICZ 6695–9	U	2001	Volvo B10M–62	Caetano Enigma	C49FT	–
2921–34	HCZ 9923–34	C*	2001	Volvo B7TL	Alex'r (B) ALX400	H49/27F	–
2935–6	HCZ 9935–6	U	2001	Volvo B7TL	Alex'r (B) ALX400	H49/27F	–
2937–40	HCZ 9937–40	C*	2001	Volvo B7TL	Alex'r (B) ALX400	H49/27F	–
701–35	HCZ 8701–35	U	2001	Scania L94	Wright Solar	B43F	–
736–38	ICZ 2736–8	U	2001	Scania L94	Wright Solar	B43F	–
87–91	ICZ 4719–23	R	2001–02	Mercedes 413Cdi	NuTrack	B12F	–
100–3	MCZ 6100–3	U	2002	Scania K114	Irizar Century	C49FT	–
1–4	OCZ 8001–4	F	2002	Mercedes 814D	Plaxton Cheetah	C24F	–
1829–37	OCZ 8829–37	F	2002–03	Optare Solo M850	Optare	B25F [6]	–
1838–72	SCZ 3838–72	U	2003	Optare Solo M850	Optare	B31F	–
2941–65	TCZ 9941–65	C	2003	Volvo B7TL	Transbus (B)	H49/27F	–
104–07	SCZ 6104–07	U	2003	Scania K114	Irizar Century	C49FT	–
108–11	SCZ 7108–11	U	2003	Scania K114	Irizar Century	C49FT	–
739–89	TCZ 1739–89	U	2003	Scania L94	Wright Solar	B43F	–
790–92	TCZ 1790–92	U	2003	Scania L94	Wright Solar	B41F	–
793–808	UCZ 8793–808	C	2003–04	Scania L94	Wright Solar	B43F	–
1661–99	TCZ 1661–99	U	2003–04	Scania K94	Irizar InterCentury	C53F	–
1700	TCZ 2700	U	2004	Scania K94	Irizar InterCentury	C53F	–
1701–06	TCZ 1701–06	U	2004	Scania K94	Irizar InterCentury	C53F	–

[1] Nos 532/3 were C53FT.
[2] No 680 was C51FT, Nos 672/3 were C49FT.
[3] Nos 2661/2 were reseated B47F in 1996, Nos 2663/4 were reseated B51F in 1996.
[4] No 1813 was converted to B22F and open rear platform in 1996.
[5] No 512 is C37FT.
[6] No 1835–7 are B24F.

(3) Pre-owned vehicles bought for Ulsterbus, Citybus and Flexibus 1989–2003

Fleet No	Reg No	Previous Reg No	Co.	New	Chassis type	Body type	Seats	Wdn

Ex-Clydeside Scottish (originally Western SMT) in 1988/9

1884	OSJ 609R		U	1976	Leyland Leopard PSU3C/4R	Alexander (F) 'Y'	B53F	n.o. t
1885	OSJ 613R		U	1976	Leyland Leopard PSU3C/4R	Alexander (F) 'Y'	B53F	1997 t
1886	OSJ 620R		U	1976	Leyland Leopard PSU3C/4R	Alexander (F) 'Y'	B53F	n.o. tp
1891	OSJ 606R		U	1976	Leyland Leopard PSU3C/4R	Alexander (F) 'Y'	B53F	n.o. rt

Ex-Northern Scottish (originally Western SMT) in 1988/9

1887	RAG 383M		U	1973	Leyland Leopard PSU3/3R	Alexander (F) 'Y'	B53F	n.o. tra
1888	RAG 388M		U	1973	Leyland Leopard PSU3/3R	Alexander (F) 'Y'	B53F	n.o. t
1889	RAG 389M		U	1973	Leyland Leopard PSU3/3R	Alexander (F) 'Y'	B53F	n.o. tr
1890	RAG 393M		U	1973	Leyland Leopard PSU3/3R	Alexander (F) 'Y'	B53F	n.o. t

Ex-Central Scottish in 1989

1881	MHS 20P		U	1976	Leyland Leopard PSU3C/3R	Alexander (F) 'Y'	B53F	n.o. t
1882	MHS 21P		U	1976	Leyland Leopard PSU3C/3R	Alexander (F) 'Y'	B53F	n.o. t
1883	MHS 22P		U	1976	Leyland Leopard PSU3C/3R	Alexander (F) 'Y'	B53F	n.o. tr

The 11 vehicles above were purchased primarily for driver training or resale. No 1885 was used in service 1996–7 only.

Ex-Sheffield and District via Eurocoach (dealer), Bexleyheath, in 1989

901	PXI 5501	JYG 417V	U*	1979	Leyland Atlantean AN68/1R	Eastern Coachworks	H43/31F	c
902	OXI 526	JYG 418V	U*	1979	Leyland Atlantean AN68/1R	Eastern Coachworks	H43/31F	1992
903	OXI 527	JYG 422V	U	1979	Leyland Atlantean AN68/1R	Eastern Coachworks	H43/31F	1992
904	OXI 514	JYG 416V	U	1979	Leyland Atlantean AN68/1R	Eastern Coachworks	H43/31F	1992
905	OXI 515	JYG 419V	U	1979	Leyland Atlantean AN68/1R	Eastern Coachworks	H43/31F	2000
906	OXI 516	JYG 420V	U	1979	Leyland Atlantean AN68/1R	Eastern Coachworks	H43/31F	1992
907	OXI 517	JYG 421V	U	1979	Leyland Atlantean AN68/1R	Eastern Coachworks	H43/31F	1998
908	OXI 518	JYG 426V	U	1979	Leyland Atlantean AN68/1R	Eastern Coachworks	H43/31F	1992
909	OXI 519	JYG 427V	U	1979	Leyland Atlantean AN68/1R	Eastern Coachworks	H43/31F	c
910	OXI 520	JYG 423V	U	1979	Leyland Atlantean AN68/1R	Eastern Coachworks	H43/31F	1992
911	OXI 528	JYG 424V	U	1979	Leyland Atlantean AN68/1R	Eastern Coachworks	H43/31F	1992
912	OXI 529	JYG 425V	U	1979	Leyland Atlantean AN68/1R	Eastern Coachworks	H43/31F	1997

Above were re-numbered to 2901–12 in 1993. 2901 was subsequently converted to glass top, 1991; 2904/6/8 to open-top, 1993; 2911 to open-top, 1997; 2912 to Wedding Bus, 1993.

Ex-North Western in 1989/90

781	OCK 345K		C	1971	Bristol RESL6L	Eastern Coachworks	B47F	n.o.
783	OCK 356K		C	1972	Bristol RESL6L	Eastern Coachworks	B47F	n.o.
784	OCK 361K		C	1972	Bristol RESL6L	Eastern Coachworks	B47F	n.o.
787	OCK 344K		C	1972	Bristol RESL6L	Eastern Coachworks	B47F	n.o.
788	OCK 358K		C	1972	Bristol RESL6L	Eastern Coachworks	B47F	1989 s
790	OCK 369K		C	1972	Bristol RESL6L	Eastern Coachworks	B47F	1990
791	OCK 370K		C	1972	Bristol RESL6L	Eastern Coachworks	B47F	n.o.
792	OCK 363K		C	1972	Bristol RESL6L	Eastern Coachworks	B47F	n.o.

Fleet No	Reg No	Previous Reg No	Co.	New	Chassis type	Body type	Seats	Wdn

Ex-Shearings, Altrincham via Plaxton (dealer), Anston, in 1989

591	OXI 521	A160 MNE	§	1984	Leyland Tiger TRCTL11/3RZ	Van Hool 'Alizee'	C53F	2001
592	OXI 522	A161 MNE	§	1984	Leyland Tiger TRCTL11/3RZ	Van Hool 'Alizee'	C53F	1999
593	OXI 523	A165 MNE	§	1984	Leyland Tiger TRCTL11/3RZ	Van Hool 'Alizee'	C53F	c
594	OXI 524	A166 MNE	§	1984	Leyland Tiger TRCTL11/3RZ	Van Hool 'Alizee'	C53F	2001
595	OXI 525	A167 MNE	§	1984	Leyland Tiger TRCTL11/3RZ	Van Hool 'Alizee'	C53F	2000

§ These vehicles were purchased by Northern Ireland Railways for operation by Ulsterbus under contract; ownership passed to Ulsterbus in 1991.

Ex-Shearings, Altrincham via Plaxton (dealer), Anston, in 1990

500	RXI 5500	B499 UNB	U	1985	Leyland Tiger TRCTL11/3RZ	Plaxton Paramount	C53F	1999
501	RXI 5501	B503 UNB	U	1985	Leyland Tiger TRCTL11/3RZ	Plaxton Paramount	C53F	1999
502	RXI 5502	B505 UNB	U	1985	Leyland Tiger TRCTL11/3RZ	Plaxton Paramount	C53F	1999
503	RXI 5503	B507 UNB	U	1985	Leyland Tiger TRCTL11/3RZ	Plaxton Paramount	C53F	1999
596	RXI 5596	B308 UNB	U	1985	Leyland Tiger TRCTL11/3RZ	Van Hool 'Alizee'	C57F	2001
597	RXI 5597	B309 UNB	U	1985	Leyland Tiger TRCTL11/3RZ	Van Hool 'Alizee'	C57F	2001
598	RXI 5598	B310 UNB	U	1985	Leyland Tiger TRCTL11/3RZ	Van Hool 'Alizee'	C57F	c

Ex-London Coaches, via Hughes DAF (dealer), Cleckheaton, in 1990

681	RXI 6681	C27 MCX	U	1986	DAF MB200DFKL	Duple Caribbean II	C49F	1993
682	RXI 6682	C29 MCX	U	1986	DAF MB200DFKL	Duple Caribbean II	C49F	2000
683	RXI 6683	C28 MCX	U	1986	DAF MB200DFKL	Duple Caribbean II	C49F	2000
685	RXI 6685	D360 PJA	U	1987	DAF MB230DFKL	Plaxton Paramount	C53F	2001

Ex-Smith's, Alcester, via Hughes DAF (dealer), Cleckheaton, in 1990

| 684 | RXI 6684 | D130 ACX | U | 1987 | DAF MB230DFKL | Duple 320SL | C57F | 2000 |

Ex-Hanmer, Wrexham, via Hughes DAF (dealer), Cleckheaton, in 1990

| 686 | RXI 6686 | D632 TLG | U | 1987 | DAF MB230DFKL | Duple 340 | C53F | 2003 |

Ex-Isaac Agnew (dealer), Belfast, in 1990 (ex-demonstration)

| 42 | MXI 6786 | | F | 1988 | Mercedes 811D | Alexander (F) 'AM' | C25F | 2003 |

Ex-M Donnell, Strabane, in 1990 (with Strabane Town Service)

| 43 | LJI 4646 | | F | 1988 | Mercedes 609D | Wright conv. | C24F | 1995 |
| 44 | MJI 3341 | | U | 1989 | Mercedes 811D | Alexander (F) 'AM' | B25F* | 2000 |

* 44 converted from B33F on acquisition.

Ex-Berryhurst International Travel Ltd, London, in 1991

| 2000 | UXI 2000 | E655 KCX | C | 1998 | DAF SBR2300DHS | Van Hool 'Astrobel' | CH57/17CT | |

Ex-Hughes, Cookstown, via Chambers (dealer), Moneymore, in 1992

| 49 | XXI 1670 | H709 OFS | F | 1991 | Mercedes 811D | PMT | C25F | 2002 |

Fleet No	Reg No	Previous Reg No	Co.	New	Chassis type	Body type	Seats	Wdn
Ex-Martyrs Memorial Free Presbyterian Church, Belfast, in August 1992									
1893	GPD 301N		U	1974	Bristol LHS6L	Eastern Coachworks	B35F	1996
1894	GPD 312N			1974	Bristol LHS6L	Eastern Coachworks	B35F	n.o.
–	NDL 770G			1970	Bristol LHS6L	Marshall	B35F	n.o.
–	NDL 771G			1970	Bristol LHS6L	Marshall	B35F	n.o.
–	MCA 611P			1976	Bristol LH6L	Eastern Coachworks	B43F	n.o.
1895	OCA 637P			1976	Bristol LH6L	Eastern Coachworks	B43F	n.o.
–	OCA 639P			1976	Bristol LH6L	Eastern Coachworks	B43F	n.o.
1892	SWS 774S		U	1978	Bristol LH6L	Eastern Coachworks	B43F	1995
–	VOI 6118				Mercedes 508D			n.o.
–	BJI 443				Commer KC	Harkness	B28F	n.o.
–	TOI 4964				Ford Transit		B14F	n.o.

These vehicles were acquired for disposal as scrap. However, two were deemed fit for use, initially for driver training and later in service. Fleet numbers were also allocated to two for cannibalisation.

Ex-Turnbull, Ettrick, in 1993

50	FAZ 3050	J823 YMS	F	1992	Mercedes 709D	Made to Measure	C26F	2001

Ex-Houston, Newtownards, in 1993

51	IBZ 3051*	H904 XGA	F	1990	Mercedes 609D	Made to Measure	C24F	2000 p

* Re-registered by previous owner.

Ex-Mercedes (demonstrator) in 1993

52	FAZ 3052	J479 XHL	U	1991	Mercedes 410D	Devon conv.	B14F	2002

Ex-Edinburgh Council, via Chambers (dealer), Moneymore, in 1994

53	OIW 6989	E637 LSF	U	1987	Mercedes 609D	Scott conv.	B16F	2001

Ex-Metropolitan Church, Whitewell, Belfast, in 1994

(14)	BIB 3383	–		1975	Ford R1114	Plaxton Supreme	C53F	n.o.
(8)	OIA 9235	GSW 235N		1975	Bedford YRT	Duple Dominant	C53F	n.o.
(16)	XIA 6577	XVU 340M		1971	Seddon Pennine IV	Seddon	B25F	n.o.
(4)	RFV 897H			1970	AEC Reliance 6MU3R	Plaxton	C53F	n.o.
(17)	GIW 9524	53 RN 17		1972	Bedford SB5	Marshall	B35F	n.o.
(15)	NJS 42S			1983	Ford R1014	Duple Dominant	C45F	n.o.
(10)	WXI 5869	AIL 7248		1970	Bedford VAS5	Alexander (B)	B29F	n.o.
(3)	HAS 952N			1975	Ford R1014	Duple Dominant	C53F	n.o.
(7)	HNU 701N			1975	Bedford YRQ	Plaxton Supreme	C45F	n.o.
(13)	RIA 8896			1983	Dodge 50	Harkness	B32F	n.o.

Numbers in brackets were fleetnumbers used by the Metropolitan Church.

Ex-McGread, Omagh, via Chambers (dealer), Moneymore, in 1994

20	CDZ 6001		U		Renault Master		B10F	1996 m

Ex-Edinburgh Council, via Chambers (dealer), Moneymore, in 1994

19	E24 JFS		F	1988	Renault Master	Aiken conv.	B11F	1999

Ex-Hertz, London, via Chambers (dealer), Moneymore, in 1994

54	FAZ 3054	E729 HLB	U	1988	Mercedes 609D	Reeve Burgess conv.	B18F	1996

Fleet No	Reg No	Previous Reg No	Co.	New	Chassis type	Body type	Seats	Wdn

Ex-Creighton, Annan, in 1984

| 55 | FAZ 3055 | G602 GOS | F | 1989 | Mercedes 609D | Scott conv. | C24F | 2000 |

Ex-Weetabix, via dealer, Victoria Bridge, in 1994

| 56 | FAZ 3056 | H643 UWE | U | 1991 | Mercedes 811D | Whittaker Europa | B26F+ | 2001 |
| 57 | FAZ 3057 | H644 UWE | U | 1991 | Mercedes 811D | Whittaker Europa | B26F+ | 2000 |

+ Converted, on acquistion, from B31F

Ex-Hertz, London, via Chambers (dealer), Moneymore, in 1994

| 58 | FAZ 3058 | F246 NLC | U | 1988 | Mercedes 609D | Reeve Burgess | B18F | 1996 |

Ex-Poots, Portadown, via Chambers (dealer), Moneymore, in 1994

| 59 | SIB 7564 | D457 SGB | F | 1987 | Mercedes 811D | Houston | C24F | 2000 |

Ex-Rose, Broadway, via Chambers (dealer), Moneymore, in 1994

| 60 | FAZ 3060 | K736 PAB | F | 1993 | Mercedes 711D | Plaxton Beaver | C25F | |

Ex-North Western, via Chambers (dealer), Moneymore, in 1994

| 61 | FAZ 3061 | F124 KAO | U | 1989 | Mercedes 609D | Reeve Burgess conv. | B24F | 1996 |
| 62 | FAZ 3062 | F127 KAO | U | 1989 | Mercedes 609D | Reeve Burgess conv. | B24F | 1998 |

Ex-demonstrator in 1994

| 2009 | IAZ 2009 | K930 EWG | C* | 1993 | Neoplan N4014NF | Neoplan | B39F | 2001 ‡ |

‡ converted to display and training unit, 2001.

Ex-Hertz, London, via Chambers (dealer), Moneymore, in 1995

| 63 | GAZ 2063 | G837 YLK | U* | 1990 | Mercedes 609D | Reeve Burgess conv. | B18F | 2001 |
| 64 | PIW 7431 | G834 YLK | F | 1990 | Mercedes 609D | Reeve Burgess conv. | C18F | 2003 |

Ex-Rose, Broadway, via Chambers (dealer), Moneymore, in 1995

| 65 | PIW 5916 | F536 DWE | F | 1988 | Mercedes 609D | Reeve Burgess | C25F | 2003 |

Ex-Poots, Portadown, via Chambers (dealer), Moneymore, in 1995

| 66 | SIB 4081 | E633 UYS | U | 1987 | Mercedes 811D | Concept conv. | C25F | 1997 |

Ex-Royal Navy, via Patterson (dealer), Ballygawley, in 1995

| 540 | HAZ 3540 | 64 KD 88 | U | 1986 | Leyland Tiger TRCTL11/3RZ | Wadham Stringer | DP52F | 1998 |

This vehicle was purchased primarily for training but was used occasionally in service.

Ex-British Airways, via Ensign (dealer), Grays, in 1996

| 2999 | RLN 233W | | U | 1981 | Leyland/DAB 36-690/4 | Roe | AB25D | n.o. t |

This vehicle was purchased primarily for training.

Ex-demonstration, via Dennison Commercials, Ballyclare, in 1996

| 2700 | HAZ 4809 | | C | 1995 | Volvo B10L | Alexander 'Ultra' | B44F | |

Ex-Chambers (dealer), Moneymore, in 1997

| A515 | GZ 6106 | | U | 1947 | Leyland Tiger PS1 | NIRTB | B34R | |

Ex-demonstration, via Dennison Commercials, Ballyclare, in 1998

| 2761 | MAZ 3761 | | C | 1996 | Volvo B10L | Alexander 'Ultra' | B44F | |

177

Fleet No	Reg No	Previous Reg No	Co.	New	Chassis type	Body type	Seats	Wdn
Ex-demonstration, via Scania UK, Milton Keynes, in 2001								
700	ECZ 9021		U	2000	Scania L94	Wright 'Solar'	B43F	
Rebuilt from Ulsterbus No 840 in 1994 as replica charabanc 'Endeavour'								
5	CZ 1988	NXI 6840	F	1989	Mercedes 709D	Wright/Ulsterbus	DP25F	

re-registered in 1996.

On hire from Mainline, Sheffield, in 1991

Fleet No	Reg No	Previous Reg No	Co.	New	Chassis type	Body type	Seats	Wdn
2001	C101 HDT		C		Leyland DAB 07-1735		AB60D	
On lease from West Midlands Travel in 1992								
45	E486 ONX		U	1987	Iveco Daily	Carlyle	B25F	1994
46	E511 TOV		F	1988	Iveco Daily	Carlyle	B25F	1994
47	E512 TOV		F	1988	Iveco Daily	Carlyle	B25F	1994
48	E513 TOV		F*	1988	Iveco Daily	Carlyle	B25F	1994
On hire from Dublin Bus in 1995								
901	94 D 29001	1994	U		CVE Omni	CVE	B14F	1995

(4a) Withdrawal dates of vehicles purchased prior to 1989 (in numerical order)

Fleet No	Regist No	Withdrawn	Fleet No	Regist No	Withdrawn	Fleet No	Regist No	Withdrawn	Fleet No	Regist No	Withdrawn	Fleet No	Regist No	Withdrawn
1	DXI 9001	1996 s	35	LXI 1035	1997	150	ROI 150	2000	252	WOI 2252	1996 m	486	IXI 1486	1996 m
2	EXI 9002	1998	36	LXI 1036	2002 s	151	TOI 151	1990 s	259	AXI 2259	2001 p	487	IXI 1487	1996 m
3	EXI 9003	1998	37	LXI 1037	1997	157	UOI 9157	1997 m	263	YOI 2263	2000 m	491	IXI 1491	1991 m
4	GXI 5004	1991	104	ROI 104	1989	158	UOI 9158	2003 a	267	YOI 2267	2000 a	534	JXI 534	2000
5	GXI 5005	1994	105	ROI 105	1997	162	UOI 9162	2003	270	YOI 2270	2003	535	JXI 535	2000
6	GXI 5006	1997	107	ROI 107	1999 r	163	UOI 9163	2003 s	293	AXI 293	1989 m	536	IXI 1536	2000 s
7	HXI 4007	1996 s	108	ROI 108	1999 r	164	UOI 9164	1989 m	300	XOI 2300	1994 m	537	GXI 537	1998 t
8	HXI 6008	1999	111	ROI 111	1993 r	165	UOI 9165	1997 m	327	BXI 327	1996 m	538	GXI 538	1994 t
9	HXI 6009	1996 s	112	ROI 112	2001	168	UOI 9168	2003 t	335	BXI 335	1995 m	539	GXI 539	1996 m
10	HXI 6010	1995	113	ROI 113	1999	169	UOI 9169	2003	346	DXI 3346	1996 m	540	RXI 5540	1991 s
11	IXI 1111	1996 s	116	ROI 116	2000	173	VOI 173	2003 s	353	DXI 3353	1994 m	541	EXI 5541	1999
12	IXI 1112	1996 s	117	ROI 117	1997 r	175	VOI 175	2003	358	DXI 3358	1990 m	542	EXI 5542	1999 s
13	IXI 3113	1996 t	118	ROI 118	2000 r	176	VOI 176	2003	360	DXI 3360	1990 m	543	EXI 5543	1999 s
14	IXI 3114	1997 s	119	ROI 119	2000	178	VOI 178	2000	362	DXI 3362	1989 m	544	EXI 5544	1999 t
15	IXI 7015	2000	120	ROI 120	1998 r	180	VOI 180	2003	364	DXI 3364	1995 m	545	EXI 5545	1996 t
16	IXI 7016	2003 s	121	ROI 121	1990 m	181	VOI 181	2003 s	375	DXI 3375	1994 m	546	EXI 5546	2003 ts
17	IXI 7017	1991 s	122	ROI 122	1992 s	182	VOI 182	2003 s	377	DXI 3377	1994 m	547	EXI 5547	1997 s
18	IXI 7018	1989 ts	123	ROI 123	1999	183	VOI 183	2003 t	382	FXI 382	2001 a	548	EXI 5548	1995 ts
19	IXI 7019	1990 ts	124	ROI 124	1997	185	VOI 185	2003	389	FXI 389	1996 m	549	EXI 5549	1999 s
20	IXI 7020	1991 ts	125	ROI 125	1997	187	VOI 187	2003	394	FXI 394	1995 m	550	EXI 5550	1999 s
21	JXI 221	1997 s	126	ROI 126	1997 r	193	VOI 193	2003	407	FXI 407	1995 f	551	BXI 5551	1999 t
22	JXI 222	1997	127	ROI 127	2003	195	VOI 195	2003	416	FXI 416	1994 m	552	BXI 5552	1999 s
23	JXI 223	1996 s	128	ROI 128	2001 a	199	VOI 199	2003	425	GXI 425	2002 a	553	BXI 5553	1999 s
24	JXI 224	1997 s	130	ROI 130	2003 t	201	VOI 201	2001 r	427	GXI 427	1996 m	554	BXI 5554	1999 ts
25	JXI 225	1997 s	135	ROI 135	2001	205	VOI 205	2003	430	GXI 430	1997 m	555	CXI 1555	1999 t
26	JXI 226	2003 p	136	ROI 136	2000	206	VOI 206	2003	435	GXI 435	1996 m	556	CXI 1556	1995 ts
27	KXI 1027	1996 s	137	ROI 137	2000	207	WOI 2207	1997 a	444	GXI 444	2001 a	557	WOI 2257	1994
28	KXI 1028	1996 s	138	ROI 138	1994 m	215	WOI 2215	1996 m	448	GXI 448	1995 a	558	WOI 2258	1995
29	KXI 1029	1997 t	140	ROI 140	2003	222	WOI 2222	2003	452	GXI 452	1996 m	559	WOI 2259	1996
30	KXI 1030	2002 s	142	ROI 142	1999	228	WOI 2228	2002 m	456	GXI 456	1996 m	560	WOI 2260	1996
32	LXI 1032	2001	144	ROI 144	1999 m	231	WOI 2231	1989 m	479	HXI 479	1997 m	561	XOI 561	1997
33	LXI 1033	1997	146	ROI 146	2003	235	WOI 2235	1991 sp	481	IXI 1481	1991 m	562	XOI 562	1996
34	LXI 1034	1997	149	ROI 149	2001	241	WOI 2241	2003 a	483	IXI 1483	1998 m	563	XOI 563	1993 s

Fleet No	Regist No	With-drawn	Fleet No	Regist No	With-drawn	Fleet No	Regist No	With-drawn	Fleet No	Regist No	With-drawn	Fleet No	Regist No	With-drawn
564	XOI 564	1992 f	1512	DOI 1512	1989 r	1934	HOI 2934	1989 s	2038	JOI 3038	1992 s	2192	POI 2192	1991 s
801	KXI 7801	1997	1559	DOI 1559	1989	1935	HOI 2935	1989 r	2043	LOI 2043	1989 m	2193	POI 2193	2193 s
802	LXI 7802	2000	1573	DOI 1573	1989	1936	KOI 9936	1989 s	2044	LOI 2044	1990 m	2194	POI 2194	1994
803	LXI 7803	1997	1578	DOI 1578	1989 s	1938	KOI 9938	1990 s	2045	LOI 2045	1991 s	2195	POI 2195	1990 m
804	KXI 7804	1996 s	1591	SOI 3591	1989 p	1939	KOI 9939	1990 s	2046	LOI 2046	1991	2196	POI 2196	1991 s
805	LXI 6805	1996 s	1714	HOI 1714	1989	1940	KOI 9940	1991 s	2052	LOI 2052	1990 s	2197	POI 2197	1991 s
806	LXI 6806	1997	1727	HOI 1727	1989 s	1941	KOI 9941	1990 s	2058	LOI 2058	1991 s	2198	POI 2198	1991 s
807	LXI 6807	1996 s	1739	HOI 1739	1989 s	1943	KOI 9943	1990 s	2059	LOI 2059	1991 s	2199	POI 2199	1997 s
808	LXI 6808	1996 s	1744	HOI 1744	1989 s	1944	KOI 9944	1990 a	2060	LOI 2060	1990	2200	POI 2200	1996
809	LXI 6809	1993 m	1745	HOI 1745	1989 ts	1945	KOI 9945	1990 s	2062	LOI 2062	1990	2201	POI 2201	1994
810	LXI 6810	2000	1746	HOI 1746	1989 s	1948	KOI 9948	1990 s	2066	LOI 2066	1989 m	2202	POI 2202	1994
811	MXI 3811	1989 m	1764	HOI 1764	1989 r	1951	KOI 9951	1991 s	2067	LOI 2067	1991 s	2203	POI 2203	1995
812	MXI 3812	1996 s	1767	HOI 1767	1989	1954	KOI 9954	1990 s	2075	LOI 2075	1991 s	2204	POI 2204	1994 a
813	MXI 3813	1996 s	1769	HOI 1769	1989 s	1955	KOI 9955	1990 s	2087	MOI 8081	1990 s	2205	POI 2205	1997 s
814	MXI 3815	2000	1788	HOI 1788	1989 s	1957	KOI 9957	1991 s	2097	MOI 8097	1991 s	2208	POI 2208	1994
815	NXI 815	1998 a	1800	HOI 800	1989 s	1958	KOI 9959	1990 s	2103	MOI 8103	1990 m	2214	ROI 2214	1992
816	NXI 816	2000	1801	LXI 4801	1996	1959	KOI 9959	1990 m	2112	MOI 8112	1989 m	2216	ROI 2216	1992
817	NXI 817	1997 s	1802	LXI 4802	1996	1960	KOI 9960	1991 s	2123	MOI 2123	1992 m	2219	ROI 2219	1990 m
818	NXI 818	2000	1803	LXI 4803	1996	1961	KOI 9961	1992 r	2126	MOI 2126	1991 s	2223	ROI 2223	1990 m
819	NXI 819	1993 m	1804	LXI 4804	1996	1962	KOI 9962	1991 s	2127	MOI 2127	1989 m	2231	ROI 2231	2000
820	NXI 820	1996	1834	LOI 1834	1989 s	1963	KOI 9963	1990 s	2128	MOI 2128	1992 m	2232	ROI 2232	2000
821	NXI 821	1996	1837	LOI 1837	1989 s	1964	KOI 9964	1991 s	2129	MOI 2129	1991 s	2233	ROI 2233	2000
822	NXI 822	1996 s	1840	LOI 1840	1989 r	1965	KOI 9965	1990 s	2131	MOI 2131	1989 m	2234	ROI 2234	1999
913	COI 913	1990 t	1841	LOI 1841	1989 r	1966	NOI 1966	1990 s	2132	MOI 2132	1989 m	2235	ROI 2235	1999
914	COI 914	1989 s	1855	LOI 1855	1989 s	1967	NOI 1967	1994 r	2133	MOI 2133	1992 m	2237	ROI 2237	1997 m
917	COI 917	1990	1858	LOI 1858	1989 s	1968	NOI 1968	1992 s	2134	MOI 2134	1992 s	2238	ROI 2238	1999
919	COI 919	1990 tp	1859	LOI 1859	1989 s	1969	NOI 1969	1992	2135	MOI 2135	1990 s	2239	ROI 2239	1996 m
924	COI 924	1990	1862	LOI 1862	1989 s	1970	NOI 1970	1991 s	2142	POI 2142	1990 s	2241	ROI 2241	1991 m
925	COI 925	1990	1863	LOI 1863	1989 s	1971	NOI 1971	1992 s	2144	POI 2144	1990 m	2242	ROI 2242	2000
939	COI 939	1989	1864	LOI 1864	1989 s	1972	NOI 1972	1992	2145	POI 2145	1990 m	2246	ROI 2246	2000
940	COI 940	1989 s	1865	LOI 1865	1989 s	1973	NOI 1973	1994	2147	POI 2147	1990 m	2247	ROI 2247	1989 m
1008	IXI 1008	1996 m	1866	LOI 1866	1989 s	1974	NOI 1974	1994	2148	POI 2148	1990 m	2249	ROI 2249	1997
1020	JXI 1020	1995 m	1867	LOI 1867	1989 s	1975	NOI 1975	1992	2149	POI 2149	1991 s	2250	ROI 2250	1999
1039	JXI 1039	1998 m	1868	LOI 1868	1989 s	1978	NOI 1978	1992 s	2151	POI 2151	1991 s	2251	ROI 2251	1997
1045	KXI 1045	1993 m	1869	LOI 1869	1989 s	1979	NOI 1979	1992 s	2153	POI 2153	1991 m	2254	ROI 2254	2000
1059	KXI 1059	1993 m	1874	LOI 1874	1989 s	1980	NOI 1980	1990 s	2154	POI 2154	1991	2255	ROI 2255	1999
1070	KXI 2070	1996 m	1875	LOI 1875	1989 r	1981	NOI 1981	1992 r	2155	POI 2155	1991 s	2256	ROI 2256	2000
1071	KXI 2071	1996 m	1876	LOI 1876	1989 s	1982	NOI 1982	1994	2156	POI 2156	1991 s	2257	ROI 2257	2000
1076	KXI 2076	1997 m	1877	LOI 1877	1989 r	1983	NOI 1983	1992 r	2159	POI 2159	1991 m	2258	ROI 2258	2000
1077	KXI 2077	1995 m	1878	LOI 1878	1990 r	1984	NOI 1984	1994	2160	POI 2160	1992 s	2259	ROI 2259	1999
1083	KXI 2083	1995 m	1880	LOI 1880	1990 s	1985	NOI 1985	1994	2161	POI 2161	1991 s	2260	ROI 2260	1997
1084	KXI 2084	1995 m	1902	HOI 1902	1989 r	1990	NOI 1990	1991	2163	POI 2163	1990 m	2261	ROI 2261	1992 m
1092	KXI 2092	1995 m	1903	HOI 1903	1989 s	1991	NOI 1991	1992	2169	POI 2169	1992 s	2262	ROI 2262	1999
1095	KXI 2095	1996 m	1904	HOI 1904	1989 r	1992	NOI 1992	1991 a	2171	POI 2171	1991 s	2264	ROI 2264	2000
1097	KXI 2097	1995 m	1905	HOI 1905	1989	1993	NOI 1993	1991 s	2172	POI 2172	1990 s	2266	ROI 2266	1999
1104	LXI 1104	1996 m	1909	HOI 1909	1989	1994	NOI 1994	1991	2173	POI 2173	1991 s	2267	ROI 2267	1999
1114	LXI 1114	1999 m	1910	HOI 1910	1989 f	1995	NOI 1995	1992 s	2174	POI 2174	1991 s	2268	ROI 2268	2000
1124	LXI 1124	1997 m	1913	HOI 2913	1990 s	1996	TOI 1996	1992 s	2175	POI 2175	1991 s	2269	ROI 2269	2000
1127	LXI 1127	1996 m	1915	HOI 2915	1989 s	1997	TOI 1997	1992 m	2176	POI 2176	1991 s	2270	ROI 2270	1997
1129	LXI 1129	1996 m	1916	HOI 2916	1989 s	1998	TOI 1998	1990 m	2177	POI 2177	1991 s	2271	TOI 2271	1990 f
1132	LXI 1132	1990 m	1917	HOI 2917	1990 s	1999	TOI 1999	1992	2178	POI 2178	1996	2272	TOI 2272	1999
1134	LXI 1134	1995 m	1918	HOI 2918	1990 s	2006	JOI 3006	1989 s	2179	POI 2179	1991 s	2273	TOI 2273	2000
1136	LXI 1136	1996 s	1919	HOI 2919	1990 s	2007	JOI 3007	1989 s	2180	POI 2180	1993 s	2275	TOI 2275	1992 a
1137	LXI 1137	1995 m	1920	HOI 2920	1990 s	2012	JOI 3012	1989 s	2181	POI 2181	1994	2276	TOI 2276	1999
1152	LXI 7152	1994 s	1921	HOI 2921	1990 s	2015	JOI 3015	1989 s	2182	POI 2182	1994	2277	TOI 2277	2000
1159	MXI 3159	1990 m	1922	HOI 2922	1990 s	2022	JOI 3022	1989 s	2183	POI 2183	1993 m	2279	TOI 2279	2000
1170	MXI 3171	1992 m	1923	HOI 2923	1989	2027	JOI 3027	1990 s	2184	POI 2184	1993	2280	TOI 2280	2000
1187	NXI 1187	1989 m	1924	HOI 2924	1990 s	2029	JOI 3029	1989 s	2185	POI 2185	1994	2281	TOI 2281	2000
1191	NXI 1191	1999 m	1925	HOI 2925	1990 s	2031	JOI 3031	1989 s	2186	POI 2186	1997	2282	TOI 2282	1990 m
1406	BOI 1406	1989	1926	HOI 2926	1990 s	2033	JOI 3033	1990 s	2187	POI 2187	1997 s	2283	TOI 2283	2000
1488	DOI 3488	1989	1927	HOI 2927	1990 s	2034	JOI 3034	1990 s	2188	POI 2188	1989 m	2284	TOI 2284	2000
1500	DOI 3500	1989	1928	HOI 2928	1990 s	2035	JOI 3035	1990 s	2189	POI 2189	1993 s	2285	TOI 2285	2000
1506	DOI 1506	1989	1932	HOI 2932	1989	2037	JOI 3037	1990 s	2190	POI 2190	1999 p	2286	TOI 2286	1997 m

Fleet No	Regist No	Withdrawn	Fleet No	Regist No	Withdrawn	Fleet No	Regist No	Withdrawn	Fleet No	Regist No	Withdrawn	Fleet No	Regist No	Withdrawn
2287	TOI 2287	2000	2358	UOI 2358	1996	2431	WOI 2431	2000	2496	XOI 2496	1997 m	2560	AXI 2560	1989 m
2288	TOI 2288	1992ap	2359	UOI 2359	1991 m	2432	WOI 2432	2003 s	2497	XOI 2497	1999	2561	BXI 2561	2001 f
2289	TOI 2289	1991 m	2360	UOI 2360	1991 m	2433	WOI 2433	2001	2498	XOI 2498	1999	2562	BXI 2562	2003 s
2290	TOI 2290	2000	2361	UOI 2361	1995	2434	WOI 2434	1997	2499	XOI 2499	2000	2563	BXI 2563	2004 s
2291	TOI 2291	2000	2362	UOI 2362	2003	2435	WOI 2435	1999	2500	XOI 2500	1999	2564	BXI 2564	2003 s
2292	TOI 2292	2000	2363	UOI 2363	1995 a	2436	WOI 2436	2001	2502	XOI 2502	1999	2565	BXI 2565	2003 p
2293	TOI 2293	2000	2366	UOI 2366	2000	2437	WOI 2437	2001	2503	XOI 2503	1997 m	2566	BXI 2566	1992 m
2294	TOI 2294	2000	2367	UOI 2367	2003 s	2438	WOI 2438	2003 p	2505	XOI 2505	2002 s	2567	BXI 2567	2003 p
2296	TOI 2296	1989 m	2368	UOI 2368	2003 s	2439	WOI 2439	1996 a	2506	XOI 2506	2003 s	2568	BXI 2568	2003 s
2297	TOI 2297	2000	2373	UOI 2373	1996 m	2440	WOI 2440	2004 s	2507	XOI 2507	1996 m	2569	BXI 2569	2004 s
2298	TOI 2298	2000	2374	UOI 2374	2003 s	2441	WOI 2441	2003 p	2508	XOI 2508	1997 m	2570	BXI 2570	2004 s
2299	TOI 2299	2000	2375	UOI 2375	2000 f	2442	WOI 2442	1996	2509	XOI 2509	2001	2571	BXI 2571	2003 s
2300	TOI 2300	2000	2376	UOI 2376	2004 s	2443	WOI 2443	2003	2510	XOI 2510	2000	2572	BXI 2572	2004
2301	TOI 2301	2001	2377	UOI 2377	2001	2444	WOI 2444	2004 p	2511	XOI 2511	2001 a	2573	BXI 2573	2004 s
2302	TOI 2302	1999	2378	UOI 2378	2000	2445	WOI 2445	1994 m	2512	XOI 2512	2003 s	2574	BXI 2574	1991 m
2304	TOI 2304	1994	2379	UOI 2379	2000	2446	WOI 2446	1997 s	2513	XOI 2513	1994 m	2575	BXI 2575	2004 s
2305	TOI 2305	2001	2380	UOI 2380	1998	2447	WOI 2447	2001	2514	XOI 2514	2003 s	2576	BXI 2576	2000 a
2306	TOI 2306	2001 p	2381	UOI 2381	2003	2449	WOI 2449	2003 s	2515	XOI 2515	1998 m	2577	BXI 2577	2003 s
2307	TOI 2307	1994	2382	UOI 2382	1999	2450	WOI 2450	2003 s	2516	XOI 2516	2003 s	2578	BXI 2578	1991 m
2308	TOI 2308	1997 m	2383	UOI 2383	1997 a	2451	WOI 2451	2003 s	2517	XOI 2517	2003	2579	BXI 2579	2003 s
2309	TOI 2309	1992 m	2384	UOI 2384	2000	2452	WOI 2452	2003 s	2519	XOI 2519	2001	2580	BXI 2580	2003 s
2310	TOI 2310	1996	2385	UOI 2385	2003 s	2453	WOI 2453	2001	2520	XOI 2520	2003 p	2581	BXI 2581	2003 s
2311	TOI 2311	2001 s	2386	UOI 2386	2001 p	2454	WOI 2454	2003 s	2521	XOI 2521	2002 s	2583	BXI 2583	2003 p
2313	TOI 2313	2000	2387	UOI 2387	2000	2455	WOI 2455	2003 s	2522	XOI 2522	2004 p	2584	BXI 2584	2003 s
2314	TOI 2314	2000	2388	UOI 2388	1997	2456	WOI 2456	2001	2523	XOI 2523	1999 a	2587	BXI 2587	1997 m
2315	TOI 2315	2000	2389	UOI 2389	2001	2457	WOI 2457	1997 s	2524	XOI 2524	2001	2588	BXI 2588	2003 s
2316	TOI 2316	2003 p	2390	UOI 2390	2003 p	2458	WOI 2458	2003	2525	XOI 2525	2003 s	2589	BXI 2589	2004 p
2317	TOI 2317	2003 a	2391	UOI 2391	1997	2459	WOI 2459	1999	2526	XOI 2526	2003 s	2590	BXI 2590	2004 p
2318	TOI 2318	2000	2392	UOI 2392	1996 m	2460	WOI 2460	2003 s	2527	XOI 2527	2004 s	2591	BXI 2591	2003 s
2319	TOI 2319	1995 a	2393	UOI 2393	1997	2462	WOI 8462	1999	2528	XOI 2528	2003	2592	BXI 2592	2003 s
2320	TOI 2320	2000 s	2394	UOI 2394	1990 m	2463	WOI 8463	1999 a	2529	XOI 2529	1989 m	2593	BXI 2593	2003 s
2321	UOI 2321	1994	2395	UOI 2395	2003 s	2465	WOI 8465	2000	2530	XOI 2530	2003 s	2594	BXI 2594	2003 s
2322	UOI 2322	1994	2397	UOI 2397	2003 s	2466	WOI 8466	1997	2531	AXI 2531	2003 p	2595	BXI 2595	2004 s
2323	UOI 2323	1990 m	2398	UOI 2398	2000	2467	WOI 8467	1997	2532	AXI 2532	2004 s	2596	BXI 2596	2004 s
2324	UOI 2324	1994 a	2399	UOI 2399	2000	2468	WOI 8468	2000	2533	AXI 2533	2003 p	2597	BXI 2597	1990 m
2326	UOI 2326	1993	2400	UOI 2400	2003 s	2469	WOI 8469	2000	2534	AXI 2534	2003 p	2598	BXI 2598	2004 s
2327	UOI 2327	1991 m	2402	VOI 8402	1996	2470	WOI 8470	1999	2535	AXI 2535	2004 s	2599	BXI 2599	2004 p
2328	UOI 2328	1994	2403	VOI 8403	1996	2471	WOI 8471	1999	2536	AXI 2536	1997 m	2600	BXI 2600	1996 m
2329	UOI 2329	1994	2404	VOI 8404	1990 m	2472	WOI 8472	2000	2537	AXI 2537	2003 s	2716	716 UZ	1993
2330	UOI 2330	1996	2405	VOI 8405	1994	2473	WOI 8473	2000	2538	AXI 2538	2003 s	2857	EOI 4857	1994 p
2331	UOI 2331	1991 m	2406	VOI 8406	1996	2474	WOI 8474	1999	2539	AXI 2539	2003 s	2858	EOI 4858	1989
2332	UOI 2332	1993 m	2408	VOI 8408	1996	2476	WOI 8476	2000	2540	AXI 2540	2003 s	2861	EOI 4861	1989
2333	UOI 2333	1996	2409	VOI 8409	1992 m	2477	WOI 8477	1999	2541	AXI 2541	2003 s	2862	EOI 4862	1989
2334	UOI 2334	1996	2410	VOI 8410	1994	2478	WOI 8478	1999	2542	AXI 2542	2003 p	2863	EOI 4863	2002 +
2335	UOI 2335	1990 m	2411	VOI 8411	1993 m	2479	WOI 8479	1999	2543	AXI 2543	2003 s	2865	EOI 4865	1989
2336	UOI 2336	1996	2412	VOI 8412	1989 m	2480	WOI 8480	1999	2544	AXI 2544	1997 a	2869	EOI 4869	1989
2337	UOI 2337	1994	2413	VOI 8413	1995	2481	XOI 2481	1999 s	2545	AXI 2545	2003 s	2893	JOI 2893	1995
2338	UOI 2338	1996 a	2414	VOI 8414	1996	2482	XOI 2482	1999	2546	AXI 2546	1997 m	3000	WOI 607	1991 s
2340	UOI 2340	1996	2415	VOI 8415	1996 p	2483	XOI 2483	1999	2547	AXI 2547	2004 s	3001	WOI 3001	1991 s
2344	UOI 2344	1994	2416	VOI 8416	1994	2484	XOI 2484	1999	2548	AXI 2548	2004 s	3002	WOI 3002	1991 s
2345	UOI 2345	1996	2417	VOI 8417	1993 m	2485	XOI 2485	1999	2549	AXI 2549	1992 m	3003	WOI 3003	1990 s
2347	UOI 2347	1991 m	2418	VOI 8418	1994	2486	XOI 2486	1999	2550	AXI 2550	2003 s	3004	WOI 3004	1990 s
2348	UOI 2348	1993	2420	VOI 8420	1994	2488	XOI 2488	1992 m	2551	AXI 2551	2003 s	3005	WOI 3005	1991 s
2350	UOI 2350	1996	2421	VOI 8421	1996	2489	XOI 2489	1999	2552	AXI 2552	2003 s	3006	HXI 3006	1991 s
2351	UOI 2351	1991 m	2423	VOI 8423	1990 m	2490	XOI 2490	1999	2553	AXI 2553	1996 m	3007	HXI 3007	1991 s
2352	UOI 2352	1994	2424	VOI 8424	1994	2491	XOI 2491	1999	2554	AXI 2554	2003 s	3008	HXI 3008	1991 s
2353	UOI 2353	1996	2425	VOI 8425	1994	2492	XOI 2492	1999	2556	AXI 2556	2003 s	3009	HXI 3009	1991 s
2354	UOI 2354	1995	2426	VOI 8426	1994	2493	XOI 2493	1999	2557	AXI 2557	1997	3010	HXI 3010	1991 s
2355	UOI 2355	1994	2428	VOI 8428	1996	2494	XOI 2494	1999	2558	AXI 2558	1991 m	3011	HXI 3011	1991 s
2356	UOI 2356	1990 m	2429	VOI 8429	1996	2495	XOI 2495	1999	2559	AXI 2559	2003 s	3012	HXI 3012	1992 s

(4b) Withdrawal dates for vehicles built new for Ulsterbus and Citybus 1989–2003

Fleet No	Regist No	Withdrawn	Fleet No	Regist No	Withdrawn	Fleet No	Regist No	Withdrawn	Fleet No	Regist No	Withdrawn
38	NXI 6938	2000 ts	835	NXI 6835	1996 m	877	TXI 7877	2003 s	1378	UXI 1378	1992 m
39	NXI 6939	1996 a	836	NXI 6836	1996 m	878	TXI 7878	1996 a	1381	WXI 4381	2002 f
40	NXI 6940	2000	837	NXI 6837	1989 m	880	TXI 7880	2003 s	1396	WXI 4396	1999 m
41	NXI 6941	2000	838	NXI 6838	1995 m	882	TXI 7882	2002	1416	WXI 4416	1997 m
515	PXI 5515	2003 t	839	NXI 6839	2003	883	AAZ 8883	2003	1423	WXI 4423	1995 m
517	PXI 5517	2003 t	840	NXI 6840	1992 m	884	AAZ 8884	2003 s	1444	XXI 1444	1999 a
521	PXI 5521	1997 m	841	NXI 6841	1993 m	886	AAZ 8886	2003 s	1455	YXI 1455	2000 a
522	PXI 5522	2003 t	842	NXI 6842	2003 s	887	AAZ 8887	2003 s	1513	DAZ 1513	1995 m
527	PXI 5527	2003 t	843	NXI 6843	2003 s	892	AAZ 8892	2003 s	1518	DAZ 1518	2000 m
530	OXI 530	2003 s	844	NXI 6844	2002	896	JAZ 3896	2001 a	1543	DAZ 1543	1995 m
532	OXI 532	2001 s	845	NXI 6845	2003	910	JAZ 3910	1997 m	1552	DAZ 1552	2003 f
611	CAZ 6611	2002 f	846	NXI 6846	2003	911	JAZ 3911	1997 m	1554	DAZ 1554	1996 m
623	CAZ 6623	1997 f	847	NXI 6847	2003 s	913	JAZ 3913	1997 m	1564	DAZ 1564	1995 m
625	CAZ 6625	1995 m	848	NXI 6848	2003 s	916	JAZ 3916	1998 a	1577	EAZ 2577	1996 m
630	CAZ 6630	2003 s	849	NXI 6849	1995 m	1023	JXI 1023	2003 f	1581	EAZ 2581	1995 m
634	CAZ 6634	2002	850	NXI 6850	2002	1219	NXI 4219	1989 m	1597	EAZ 2597	2000 f
635	CAZ 6635	2002 f	851	NXI 6851	2003 s	1222	NXI 4222	1995 m	1618	JAZ 1618	1996 m
637	CAZ 6637	2003 s	852	NXI 6852	2003	1230	NXI 4230	1990 m	1807	SXI 2807	2002 s
638	CAZ 6638	1996 m	853	NXI 6853	2003 s	1231	NXI 4231	1990 m	1809	SXI 2809	2003 s
673	UXI 1673	2003 ts	855	NXI 6855	2003 s	1237	NXI 4237	1999 f	2602	LXI 6602	2001 a
674	UXI 1674	2003 s	857	NXI 6857	1989 m	1240	NXI 4240	1992 m	2617	NXI 4617	1992 m
675	UXI 1675	2003 s	858	NXI 6858	1994 m	1264	OXI 1264	1995 m	2622	NXI 4622	1994 m
676	UXI 1676	2003 ts	859	NXI 6859	2003 s	1266	OXI 1266	1994 m	2632	NXI 4632	1990 m
678	SXI 1678	2003 as	860	NXI 6860	2003 s	1283	OXI 1283	1996 m	2633	NXI 4633	1996 m
823	NXI 6823	2002 s	862	NXI 6862	2003	1284	OXI 1284	1996 m	2637	SXI 2637	1991 m
824	NXI 6824	2003	864	TXI 7864	2003 s	1289	OXI 1289	1993 m	2652	SXI 2652	1997 m
825	NXI 6825	2003 s	868	TXI 7868	1996 m	1305	PXI 1305	1996 m	2713	LAZ 2713	2000 m
826	NXI 6826	2003	869	TXI 7869	2003	1307	PXI 1307	1996 m	2728	LAZ 2728	2001 m
828	NXI 6828	2003 s	870	TXI 7870	2003 s	1308	PXI 1308	1996 m	2735	LAZ 2735	1999 m
829	NXI 6829	2000	871	TXI 7871	2003 s	1314	PXI 1314	1996 m	2736	LAZ 2736	1997 m
831	NXI 6831	2003	874	TXI 7874	2003 s	1329	RXI 3329	1993 m	2779	BCZ 2779	2001 m
832	NXI 6832	2003 s	875	TXI 7875	2003 s	1334	RXI 3334	1998 m			
833	NXI 6833	2003	876	TXI 7876	2003 s	1361	UXI 1361	1997 m			

(4c) Withdrawal dates of pre-owned vehicles acquired by Ulsterbus and Citybus before 1989. (For full details of these vehicles, and the fleet of second-hand Bristol REs, please refer to Buses in Ulster vols. 4 and 5)

Fleet No	Regist No	Withdrawn	Fleet No	Regist No	Withdrawn	Fleet No	Regist No	Withdrawn	Fleet No	Regist No	Withdrawn
31	CDZ 6664	2001	697	HIB 9482	1999 s	965	GGG 303N	1990	984	SSF 394H	1991
565	AJD 165T	1992 s	900	WFS 280K	1991 s	966	GGG 305N	1989	988	SSF 388H	1989 s
566	VLB 666M	1989	903	WFS 296K	1989	971	JGA 203N	1992	995	WFS 275K	1989 s
576	AJD 166T	1992 ts	956	MDS 669P	1992 s	972	KSU 831P	1991	996	WFS 276K	1989
690	HIB 9642	1989 t	957	KSU 865P	1992 s	975	OYS 199M	1991 s	998	WFS 278K	1989 t
694	DIB 2835	1989	960	KSU 872P	1991	979	SSF 371H	1989	999	WFS 289K	1990
695	FIB 4533	1989 s	961	KSU 873P	1990	981	SSF 377H	1989	1892	SHS 962M	1989 s
696	FIB 8279	1990 s	963	JUS 776N	1990 t	983	SSF 393H	1991			

(4d) Withdrawal dates of pre-owned vehicles acquired by Ulsterbus and Citybus after 1989

Fleet No	Regist No	Withdrawn	Fleet No	Regist No	Withdrawn	Fleet No	Regist No	Withdrawn	Fleet No	Regist No	Withdrawn
19	E24 JFS	1999	56	FAZ 3056	2001	592	OXI 522	1999s	905	OXI 515	1992s
20	CDZ 6001	1996m	57	FAZ 3057	2000s	594	OXI 524	2001	(2)906	OXI 516	1998
42	MJI 6786	2003s	58	FAZ 3058	1996	595	OXI 525	2000s	907	OXI 517	1992
43	LJI 4646	1995m	59	SIB 7564	2000	596	RXI 5596	2001ts	909	OXI 519	1992s
44	MJI 3441	2000s	61	FAZ 3061	1996	597	RXI 5597	2001t	910	OXI 520	1992s
45	E486 ONX	1994	62	FAZ 3062	1998s	598	RXI 5598	2001t	(2)912	OXI 529	1997a
46	E511 TOV	1994	63	GAZ 2063	2001	681	RXI 6681	1993t	1881	MHS 20P	no t
47	E512 TOV	1994	64	PIW 7431	2003s	682	RXI 6682	2000ts	1882	MHS 21P	no t
48	E513 TOV	1994	65	PIW 5916	2003s	683	RXI 6683	2000	1883	MHS 22P	no t
49	XXI 1670	2002s	66	SIB 4081	1987	684	RXI 6684	2000	1892	SWS 774S	1995p
50	FAZ 3050	2001s	500	RXI 5500	1999s	685	RXI 6685	2001ts	1893	GPD 301N	1996p
51	IBZ 3051	2000p	501	RXI 5501	1999s	686	RXI 6686	2003ts	2009	IAZ 2009	2001
52	FAZ 3052	2002s	502	RXI 5502	1999s	901	94 D 29001	1995	2999	RLN 233W	no t
53	OIW 6989	2001s	503	RXI 5503	1999	(2)902	OXI 526	1992			
54	FAZ 3054	1996	540	HAZ 3540	1998ts	903	OXI 527	1992s			
55	FAZ 3055	2000	591	OXI 521	2001ts	(2)904	OXI 514	2000m			

(5) Vehicles re-registered 1988–2003

Fleet Nr	Former Reg Nr	New Reg Nr	Date	Fleet Nr	Former Reg Nr	New Reg Nr	Date	Fleet Nr	Former Reg Nr	New Reg Nr	Date
5	NXI 6840	CZ 1988	3/96	108	ROI 108	SCZ 2658	4/03	195	VOI 195	UCZ 5421	10/03
11	IXI 1111	WIW 4624	10/98	109+	ROI 109	WAZ 5652	8/98	199	VOI 199	KCZ 4583	8/01
22	JXI 222	TAZ 3731	12/97	111	ROI 111	TBZ 8399	5/98	222*	WOI 2222	SCZ 5503	4/03
50	J823 YMS	FAZ 3050	11/94	117	ROI 117	YAZ 6412	2/99	444*	GXI 444	JCZ 2226	4/01
52	J479 XHL	FAZ 3052	11/94	118	ROI 118	ICZ 3919	3/01	540+	B272 AMG	RXI 5540	3/90
54	E729 HLB	FAZ 3054	11/94	119*	ROI 119	HCZ 1770	11/00	591	OXI 521	JCZ 5225	6/01
55	G622 GOS	FAZ 3055	11/94	120	ROI 120	HCZ 5695	1/01	2300*	TOI 2300	GCZ 6199	9/00
56	H643 UWE	FAZ 3056	11/94	128*	ROI 128	LCZ 9742	1/02	2904*	OXI 514	GCZ 1804	7/00
57	H644 UWE	FAZ 3057	11/94	135*	ROI 135	LCZ 7113	1/02				
58	F246 NLC	FAZ 3058	11/94	146*	ROI 146	UCZ 7654	12/03	*re-registered on paper only; vehicle already withdrawn			
60	K736 PAB	FAZ 3060	11/94	150*	ROI 150	HCZ 1886	11/00				
63	G837 YLK	GAZ 2063	5/95	182*	VOI 182	UCZ 1781	9/03				
107	ROI 107	CCZ 5919	10/99	186	VOI 186	OCZ 4209	7/02				

(6) Vehicles re-numbered 1988–2003

Fleet Nr	Reg Nr	New Fleet Nr	Date	Fleet Nr	Reg Nr	New Fleet Nr	Date	Fleet Nr	Reg Nr	New Fleet Nr	Date
107	CCZ 5919 (ROI 107)	4107	3/03	126	ROI 126	4126	3/03	908	OXI 518 (JYG 426V)	2908	9/95
108	SCZ 2658 (ROI 108)	4108	3/03	199	KCZ 4583 (VOI 199)	4199	3/03	911	OXI 528 (JYG 424V)	2911	9/95
109	WAZ 5652 (ROI 109)	4109	3/03	533	OCS 733	9533	4/89	912	OXI 529 (JYG 425V)	2912	9/95
111	TBZ 8399 (ROI 111)	4111	3/03	537	OCS 737	9537	4/89	1512	DOI 1512	9512	9/94
117	YAZ 6412 (ROI 117)	4117	3/03	540	OCS 740	9540	4/89	3000	DAZ 3000	3110	11/03
118	ICZ 3919 (ROI 118)	4118	3/03	901	PXI 5501 (JYG 417V)	2901	9/95	3001	DAZ 3001	3111	11/03
120	HCZ 5695 (ROI 120)	4120	3/03	902	OXI 526 (JYG 418V)	2902	9/95	3002	JAZ 3002	3112	11/03
				904	OXI 514 (JYG 416V)	2904	9/95	3003	JAZ 3003	3113	11/03
				906	OXI 516 (JYG 420V)	2906	9/95				

(8) Vehicles retained for towing after withdrawal

Leyland Leopard L1
(ex Western SMT)
(9)533	10/77–10/92	DP
(9)537	11/77–12/91	CG
(9)540	11/80–2/90	NY

Leyland Leopard
584	6/80–5/94	E

Bristol LH6L
1604	7/87–1/89	BG
1636	6/86–7/89	NA
1637	6/86–3/93	NC;
	3/93–7/95	DP

Bedford YRQ
1706	11/88–5/89	LB
1716	7/85–6/95	AM
1717	12/84–9/94	F

1735	4/83–1/92	OM
1748	8/82–6/91	V
1751	10/82–4/02	MF
1753	10/82–11/90	DG
1757	4/89–4/92	NB
1758	7/85–2/99	BM
1763	12/84–12/93	SS
1764	7/91–8/94	V
1773	10/85–10/89	LD
1784	12/84–1/93	AD
1790	4/88–6/90	OX;
	6/90–7/90	NB
1793	10/88–2/95	LR

Bedford YLQ
1840	12/90–9/97f	DG
1841	10/89–5/94	LD;
	5/94–5/96	E
1843	5/88–1/94	AT

1860	3/89–1/93	BG
1875	7/89–1/97	NA
1877	5/89–9/92	LB;
	9/92–10/95	BG
1878	2/90–2/95	NY;
	6/95–8/06p	AM

Leyland Leopard
1512	w/d 89;	
	4/92–4/98	NB;
	4/98–10/99	NA
1902	5/94–c	LD
1904	12/92–c	LB
1935	11/93–c	SS
1961	2/95–c	NY
1967	8/96–12/02	BG;
	12/02–c	NA
1981	9/94–c	F
1983	8/94–c	V

(4)107	9/99–c	AT
(4)108	5/02–c	MF
(4)111	6/96–c	DP
(4)117	4/98–c	NB
(4)118	1/01–c	OM
(4)120	11/00–c	LR
(4)126	3/98–c	DG
(4)199	3/04–c	LD

Leyland Leopard
(ex Scottish Group)
1882	2/99– c	BM
1883	1/92–2/00	OM
1884	8/91–4/93	LR
1887	7/91–3/93a	DP
1889	2/95–10/99	LR
1890	1/92–c	CG
1891	5/96–c	E

(9) Vehicles allocated for Driver Training

Leyland Atlanteans:
913	5/90 –9/90	
919	5/90–5/90p	
963	4/90–4/90	
971	11/89–2/91	
not continuous; reverted to service.		
977	11/85–2/89	
984	1/89–5/89	
	reverted to service.	
997	3/87–4/89s	
998	6/89–10/89	

Bristol LH & LHS
1629	7/87–6/89p	
1638	4/88–7/89	
1687	7/88–9/94	
1692	1/88–6/89	
1699	3/87–3/93	
1892	5/93–9/95	
not continuous; returned to service		
1893	6/93–3/95	
not continuous; returned to service		

Bedford YRT/YRQ/YLQ
690	4/89–9/95s	
	not continuous	
1745	9/89–10/89	
1831	1/86–3/94	

Bristol RELL
714	3/89–8/90	
778	4/89–8/90	
779	4/89–8/90	
785	4/89–8/90	
2275	2/90–4/90	
	returned to service	
2437	9/01–4/02	
	Wayfarer training unit	

2447	9/01–4/02
	Wayfarer training unit
2524	9/01–4/02
	Wayfarer training unit

Leyland Leopard
168	11/03 – c
183	9/03–10/03
187	8/03–8/03
	returned to service
259	3/95–1/01
	not continuous
576	2/90– 2/95
	not continuous
1568	11/87–11/90s

Leyland Leopard
(ex Scottish Bus Group)
1881	7/89–10/99
	not continuous
1882	7/89–4/97r
	not continuous
1883	7/89–7/90r
1884	9/89 – 11/99p
1885	9/89–10/96
	returned to service
1886	10/88–2/97p
1887	5/89–7/90r
1888	10/88–7/89
1889	5/89–1/93r
1890	4/89–11/90r
1891	10/88–2/96r

Leyland DAB
(bought for training but little used)
2999	3/96– 3/97

Leyland Tiger
352	1/90–10/90
	returned to service
515	5/02–c not continuous
517	5/02– c not continuous
522	5/02–c not continuous
527	5/02–c not continuous
530	6/02–3/03s
not continuous; returned to service	
537	1/94–8/02s
	not continuous
538	9/94–1/03s
	not continuous
540	7/95–1/02s
	not continuous
544	7/98–6/00
	not continuous
545	1/96–6/01
546	4/96–5/03s
547	1/97–1/03s
548	1/95–1/03s
551	2/00–4/00
554	6/98–1/00s
	not continuous
555	7/98–3/00
	not continuous
556	1/95–8/99s
	not continuous
591	6/01– 4/05s
596	1/01– 8/05s
597	7/01–12/03
598	11/01–c
2605	7/02–8/02
	returned to service

Daimler Fleetline
2825	5/83–4/89
2863	6/88–4/89
	returned to service

DAF
670	8/03–8/03
	returned to service
671	8/03–8/03
	returned to service
673	8/03–6/04
674	5/02–6/02
	returned to service
676	9/03–3/04s
681	11/93–8/00
682	1/00–8/03s
685	5/01–6/02s
686	1/00–8/03s
	not continuous
697	9/94–10/97
	returned to service

Mercedes
13	1/98–6/98
29	7/98–5/00
38	5/00–6/02s

Fiat
17	1/90–8/90
	returned to service
18	9/89–3/91s
19	8/90–3/91s

(10) Vehicles allocated for staff transport

1521	11/87–10/89s	
1935	10/89–8/91r	

(7) Demonstrators

Fleet No	Reg. No	Chassis	Body	Period of loan	Notes
42	MXI 6786	Mercedes 811D	Alexander 'AM'	10/88–06/89	Purchased 1990
898	E456 VUM	Talbot Express		??/89	
899	D274 SMA	Dodge	Alexander	??/89	
–	F370 BUA	DAF	Optare Delta	??/89	Not operated
–	F516 OKV	Talbot Pullman		02/89	
–	F369 TVN	CVE Omni		05/89	Not operated
–	F787 VPY	CVE Omni		05/89	Not operated
–	G737 NNS	Mercedes 709D	Wright 'TS'	10/89	Displayed at NEC
100	G541 JBV	Dennis Dart	Duple	03/90	
100	F321 HHR	Dennis Javelin	Duple 320	05/90	
2002	G910 XFC	DAF SB220	Optare Delta	03/92	
2003	J110 SPB	Dennis Lance	Alexander 'PS'	03/92	
2004	H912 HRO	Scania N113CRB	Plaxton Verde	03/92	
–	VP 18 HK	DAF SBR220	Den Oudsten	07/92	Inspected
2005	K473 EDT	Mercedes O405	Alexander 'PS'	11/92 & 02/93	
1800	LDZ 6040	Dennis Dart	Wright Handybus	12/92	
2006	K247 HKV	Volvo B10B	Northern Counties	03/93	
2007	K891 XGS	Iveco TurboCity 50	Alexander	05/93	
2008	L25 LSX	Scania MaxCi	East Lancs	03/94–05/94	
2009	K930 EWG	Neoplan N4014	Neoplan	09/94–12/94	Purchased
2010	M310 KHP	Volvo B10B	Wright	01/95	
2700	HAZ 4809	Volvo B10L	Alexander Ultra	08/95–03/96	Purchased
2011	M918 MRW	Volvo B6LE	Wright Crusader	11/95	
2761	MAZ 3761	Volvo B10L	Alexander Ultra	09/96–04/98	Purchased
2012	P443 SWX	Optare Excel		11/97	
2013	R460 VOP	Volvo B10BLE	Wright Renown	11/97–01/98	
2014	R739 TMO	Dennis Dart	Plaxton Super Pointer	02/98–04/98	
2015	S376 MVP	Volvo B10BLE	Alexander	09/98–10/98	
2016	S350 SET	Scania Axcess	Wright Floline	09/98–10/98	
–	TP 028 RJ	Mercedes O405N	Mercedes	03/99	Not operated
–	T343 FWR	OptareSolo		??/99	Inspected
2017	T222 MTB	MAN	Alexander ALX300	09/99–11/99	
2018	W438 CWX	Optare Excel II		05/00	
2019	V929 FMS	Dennis Trident	Alexander ALX400	12/99	
2020	V928 FMS	Dennis Dart SLF	Alexander ALX200	12/99	Not operated
2021	ECZ 9021	Scania L94	Wright Solar	05/00–05/01	Purchased
–	AKZ 7122	Dennis Dart SLF	Wright Crusader	09/00	Battery bus
2022	W38 DOE	Volvo B7R	Plaxton Prima	09/00–11/00	
2023	GCZ 9023	Volvo B7L	Wright Eclipse	02/01–12/01	
2024	X157 JOP	Volvo B7TL	Plaxton President	11/00–04/01	
2025	Y652 CCX	Electrocity	Wright Cadet	06/02	VDL chassis
–	Unreg'd	Scania L94 (x2)	Irizar InterCentury	11/02	Inspected
–	Unreg'd	Volvo B7R (x2)	Plaxton Prima	11/02	Inspected
2026	DJ03 EVM	Dennis Trident	Alexander ALX400	08/03	Not operated